Wise Words and Quotes

Vern McLellan

TYNDALE HOUSE PUBLISHERS, INC. | CAROL STREAM, ILLINOIS

Visit Tyndale's exciting Web site at www.tyndale.com

TYNDALE and Tyndale's quill logo are registered trademarks of Tyndale House Publishers, Inc.

Wise Words and Quotes

Edited by Anne Goldsmith

Designed by Justin Ahrens

Published in association with the literary agency of Alive Communications, Inc., 7680 Goddard Street, Suite 200, Colorado Springs, CO 80920.

This is an updated version of The Complete Book of Sensible Sayings & Wacky Wit, which was published in 1998 under ISBN-13: 978-0-8423-5129-4.

Library of Congress Cataloging-in-Publication Data

The complete book of wise words & quotes / [edited by] Vernon McLellan.
   p. cm.
   ISBN-13: 978-0-8423-3671-0 (pbk.: alk. paper)
   ISBN-10: 0-8423-3671-0 (pbk.: alk. paper)
   1. Quotations, English. 2. Proverbs. I. McLellan, Vernon K.

PN6081.C585 2000
082—dc21   99-042253

Printed in the United States of America

13 12 11 10 09 08 07
16 15 14 13 12 11 10

To Lorie
*with pride and appreciation
A delightful daughter . . .
A magnificent mother.*

CONTENTS

Accomplishment

If you wait for perfect conditions, you will never get anything done. Be sure to stay busy and plant a variety of crops, for you never know which will grow—perhaps they all will.

ECCLESIASTES 11:4, 6

Whatever you do, do well. For when you go to the grave, there will be no work or planning or knowledge or wisdom.

ECCLESIASTES 9:10

Accomplishment

The most agreeable thing in life is worthy accomplishment.

EDGAR ROWE

You can't build your reputation on what you're going to do.

HENRY FORD

No matter what your lot in life, build something on it.

Lord, grant that I may always desire more than I can accomplish.

MICHELANGELO

Every man who is high up loves to think he has done it all himself; and his wife smiles, and lets it go at that.

JAMES BARRIE

He who putters around winds up in the hole.

The Difficult is that which can be done immediately;
The Impossible is that which takes a little longer.

GEORGE SANTAYANA

If your mind can conceive it, and your heart can believe it, then you can achieve it.

I have fought a good fight, I have finished the race, and I have remained faithful.

THE APOSTLE PAUL, 2 TIMOTHY 4:7

Definiteness of purpose is the starting point of all achievement.

CLEMENT STONE

Unless you try to do something beyond what you have already mastered, you will never grow up.

RONALD E. OSBORN

Action

Then the Lord said to Moses, "Why are you crying out to me? Tell the people to get moving!"

EXODUS 14:15

Action

Everything comes to him who hustles while he waits.

THOMAS EDISON

Roadside sign in Kentucky: "Pray for a good harvest, but keep on hoeing!"

Did is a word of achievement,
   Won't is a word of retreat,
Might is a word of bereavement,
   Can't is a word of defeat,
Ought is a word of duty,
   Try is a word each hour,
Will is a word of beauty,
   Can is a word of power.

The thing to try when all else fails is again. Giving it another try is better than an alibi.

Deliberation is the work of many men. Action, of one alone.

CHARLES DE GAULLE

Action should not be confused with haste.   LEE IACOCCA

He who believes is strong; he who doubts is weak. Strong convictions precede great actions.   J. F. CLARKE

Don't find fault. Find a remedy.   HENRY FORD

God, save us from hotheads who lead us to act foolishly, and from cold feet that would keep us from acting at all.

PETER MARSHALL

Don't stand shivering upon the bank; plunge in at once, and have it over with. SAM GLICK

People forget how fast you did a job—but they remember how well you did it. HOWARD W. NEWTON

Progress always involves risk; you can't steal second base and keep your foot on first. FREDERICK WILCOX

Adaptability

It is pleasant to see dreams come true,
but fools will not turn from evil to
attain them.

PROVERBS 13:19

The godly give good advice to their
friends; the wicked lead them astray.

PROVERBS 12:26

Adaptability

Most people are willing to adapt not because they see the light but because they feel the heat.

Sign on a pastor's desk: "It's too late to agree with me, I've already changed my mind!"

The past is a guidepost, not a hitching post.

L. THOMAS HOLDCROFT

If you don't like the weather in New England, just wait a few minutes. MARK TWAIN

The most significant change in a person's life is a change of attitude. Right attitudes produce right actions.

WILLIAM J. JOHNSON

The foolish and the dead alone never change their opinions.

JAMES R. LOWELL

It is well for people to change their minds occasionally in order to keep them clean. LUTHER BURBANK

When you're through changing, you're through. BRUCE BARTON

The bamboo which bends is stronger than the oak which resists. JAPANESE PROVERB

Many people hate any change that doesn't jingle in their pocket.

The world changes so fast that you couldn't stay wrong all the time if you tried.

Adversity

If you fail under pressure, your strength is not very great. Don't raid the house where the godly live. They may trip seven times, but each time they will rise again. But one calamity is enough to lay the wicked low.

PROVERBS 24:10, 15-16

Adversity

He who wants a place in the sun should expect blisters.

It takes both rain and sunshine to make a rainbow.

It's easy enough to be pleasant
When everything goes like a song;
But the man worthwhile
Is the man who can smile
When everything's going dead wrong.

It takes two things to blow down a tree: a heavy wind outside and rot and decay inside. So it is with man. The winds of adversity may cause him to bend, but if he's strong and vigorous within, he will arise and grow to new heights after the storm passes.

Sometimes you find you're up against it because you back up instead of going ahead.

Prosperity makes friends; adversity tries them.

Adversity causes some men to break and others to break records.

Adversity is a gathering cloud putting on its thunderwear.

He knows not his own strength who has not met adversity. Heaven prepares good men with crosses.

The gem cannot be polished without friction nor the child of God cleansed without adversity.

As you look back over your years of marriage, you will undoubtedly discover that some of your most meaningful and special times were marked by adversity. Shared together, tough circumstances cement a relationship and give it new depth. Instead of shrinking from adversity and griping about it, we should capitalize on its potential for strengthening our family life. JOHN DOBBERT

When the going gets tough, the tough get going.
ROBERT SCHULLER

Aging

Even in old age they will still produce
fruit; they will remain vital and green.
They will declare, "The Lord is just!
He is my rock! There is nothing but
goodness in him!"

PSALM 92:14-15

———

Gray hair is a crown of glory; it is
gained by living a godly life. The
glory of the young is their strength;
the gray hair of experience is the
splendor of the old.

PROVERBS 16:31; 20:29

Aging

Age occurs when you find yourself using one bend-over to pick up two things.

You're getting older when, while tying your shoelace, you ask yourself the question: "What else can I do while I'm down here?"

When people tell you how young you look, they are also telling you how old you are. CARY GRANT

Age is a sorry traveling companion. DANISH PROVERB

When a woman tells you her age it's all right to look surprised, but don't scowl. WILSON MIZNER

The woman who tells her age is either too young to have anything to lose or too old to have anything to gain.
CHINESE PROVERB

When you were born, you cried and the world rejoiced. Live your life in such a way that when you die, the world will cry and you will rejoice.

The ten best years of a woman's life are between the ages of twenty-nine and thirty. PETER WEISS

You know you're over the hill when you develop a taste for bran flakes.

He whose night out is followed by a day in is growing old.

I'm not over the hill; I'm on the back nine.

Forty is the old age of youth, and fifty is the youth of old age.

12

To me, old age is always fifteen years older than I am.

BERNARD BARUCH

Age is a question of mind over matter. If you don't mind, it doesn't matter.

SATCHEL PAIGE

When you're over the hill, your speed picks up.

Old minds are like old horses; you must exercise them if you wish to keep them in working order.

JOHN ADAMS

Life gets more enjoyable the older you get. The hardest years in life are between ten and seventy.

HELEN HAYES

If you want to know how old a woman is, ask her sister-in-law.

The principal objection to old age is that there's no future in it.

One cannot help being old, but one can resist being aged.

You're an old-timer if you remember when castor oil and camphor were the miracle drugs.

There are three things that grow more precious with age: old wood to burn, old books to read, and old friends to enjoy.

There's many a good tune in an old fiddle!

You can tell you are growing older when . . .

> You get winded playing checkers.
> Your children begin to look middle-aged.
> You look forward to a dull evening.
> You know all the answers, but nobody's asking the questions.
> You join the health club—and don't go.
> You sit in a rocking chair and can't get it going.

Your knees buckle, and your belt won't.
You burn the midnight oil at 9:00 P.M.
Dialing long distance wears you out.
Your back goes out more often than you do.
The little gray-haired lady you help across the street is your wife.
You have too much room in the house and not enough in the medicine cabinet.
You sink your teeth into a steak, and they stay there.
Everything hurts, and what doesn't hurt doesn't work.
You can't stand people who are intolerant.

Anger

A gentle answer turns away wrath, but
harsh words stir up anger.

PROVERBS 15:1

People with good sense restrain their
anger; they earn esteem by
overlooking wrongs.

PROVERBS 19:11

Anger

Anger is just one letter short of danger.

Hot words never resulted in cool judgment.

Those who control their anger have great understanding;
those with a hasty temper will make mistakes.

SOLOMON, PROVERBS 14:29

He who has a sharp tongue soon cuts his own throat.

The greatest remedy for anger is delay.

When a man is wrong and won't admit it, he always becomes
angry.

If you speak when you're angry, you'll make the best speech
you'll ever regret.

When you see a married couple coming down the street, the
one who is two or three steps ahead is the one who's mad.

When angry, count to ten before you speak; if very angry,
count to a hundred. THOMAS JEFFERSON

Anger is momentary madness, so control your passion or it
will control you. HORACE

Anger makes your mouth work faster than your mind.

Every time you give someone a piece of your mind you make
your head a little emptier.

Anger is a wind that blows out the lamp of the mind.

Blowing your stack adds to air pollution.

Animals

The godly are concerned for the welfare of their animals, but even the kindness of the wicked is cruel.

PROVERBS 12:10

————

My sheep recognize my voice; I know them, and they follow me. I give them eternal life, and they will never perish.

JESUS, JOHN 10:27-28

Animals

Dogs come when they're called; cats take a message and get back to you.

It may be that one reason a dog is a good friend is that his tail wags and not his tongue.

Young kangaroos grow by leaps and bounds.

They say a reasonable number of fleas is good for a dog—it keeps him from brooding over being a dog.   E. N. WESTCOTT

The reason a dog is man's best friend is because he does not pretend, he proves it.

No horse gets anywhere until it is harnessed.

A mule makes no headway when it is kicking.

A camel is a warped horse. A horse is an oatsmobile.

You can lead a horse to water, but you can't make it drink.

If you growl all day, it's natural to feel dog-tired at night.

The reason the cow jumped over the moon was because there was a short circuit in the milking machine.

The cow is of the bovine ilk;
One end is moo, the other milk.   OGDEN NASH

Milk the cow which is near. Why pursue the one which runs away?   THEOCRITUS

Never swap horses while crossing a stream.

She was as contented as a cow in a cornfield.

He who wants milk should not set himself in the middle of a pasture waiting for a cow to back up to him.

Babies

You have taught children and nursing infants to give you praise. They silence your enemies who were seeking revenge.

PSALM 8:2

You must crave pure spiritual milk so that you can grow into the fullness of your salvation. Cry out for this nourishment as a baby cries for milk, now that you have had a taste of the Lord's kindness.

1 PETER 2:2-3

Then Jesus prayed this prayer: "O Father, Lord of heaven and earth, thank you for hiding the truth from those who think themselves so wise and clever, and for revealing it to the childlike."

MATTHEW 11:25

Babies

A baby is God's opinion that the world should go on.

CARL SANDBURG

Babies are angels whose wings grow shorter as their legs grow longer.

Babies are little rivets in the bonds of marriage.

A perfect example of minority rule is a baby in the house.

Babies are such a nice way to start people.

DON HEROLD

One grandmother will spoil a baby. Two working together will bring him up in the way he should go, for each will suspect the other of spoiling him and will check it.

ALLAN WHITE

The art of being a parent is to sleep when the baby isn't looking.

Adam and Eve had many advantages, but the principal one was that they escaped teething.

MARK TWAIN

A baby is born with a need to be loved—and never outgrows it.

FRANK A. CLARK

Every baby born into the world is a finer one than the last.

CHARLES DICKENS

Feeding a baby is one sure way of finding out how badly your suit spots.

A soiled baby with a neglected nose cannot consciously be regarded as a thing of beauty.

MARK TWAIN

A baby is a loud noise at one end and no sense of
responsibility at the other. RONALD KNOX

Out of the mouth of babes comes a lot of what they should
have swallowed. FRANKLIN P. JONES

A baby is a bald head and a pair of lungs. EUGENE FIELD

Bravery

Be strong and courageous! Do not be afraid of them! The Lord your God will go ahead of you. He will neither fail you nor forsake you.

DEUTERONOMY 31:6

So be strong and take courage, all you who put your hope in the Lord!

PSALM 31:24

The human spirit can endure a sick body, but who can bear it if the spirit is crushed?

PROVERBS 18:14

The wicked run away when no one is chasing them, but the godly are as bold as lions.

PROVERBS 28:1

Bravery

The wishbone will never replace the backbone.   WILL HENRY

He who lacks courage thinks with his legs.

Success is never final. Failure is never fatal. It's courage that counts.   COACH JOHN WOODEN

Behold the turtle. He makes progress only when he sticks his neck out.   JAMES B. CONANT

Bravery is the capacity to perform properly even when scared half to death.   OMAR BRADLEY

Courage is fear that has said its prayers.

He who does not dare will not get his share.

There's only a slight difference between keeping your chin up and sticking your neck out, but it's a difference worth knowing.

Have courage for the great sorrows of life and patience for the small ones; and when you have laboriously accomplished your daily task, go to sleep in peace. God is awake.   VICTOR HUGO

Don't be afraid to take a big step if one is indicated. You can't cross a chasm in two small jumps.   DAVID LLOYD GEORGE

Act brave. The world steps aside for the man who acts like he knows where he is going.   D. S. JORDAN

A man of courage is also full of faith.   CICERO

When there is no money, half is gone; when there is no courage, all is gone.

Don't consult a coward about war.

You'd be surprised how often nerve succeeds.

To the brave and true, nothing is difficult.

Lord, grant me the serenity to accept the things I cannot change, the courage to change the things I can, and the wisdom to know the difference. REINHOLD NIEBUHR

It is easy to be brave from a safe distance. AESOP

It's courage and character that make the difference between players and great players, between great surgeons and ones who bury their mistakes. COACH PETE CARROL

Courage is the quality of mind that makes us forget how afraid we are.

Courage isn't a brilliant dash,
A daring deed in a moment's flash;
It isn't an instantaneous thing
Born of despair with a sudden spring.
But it's something deep in the soul of man
That is working always to serve some plan. EDGAR A. GUEST

Courage is the first of human qualities because it is the quality which guarantees all others. WINSTON CHURCHILL

Bravery is falling but not yielding. LATIN PROVERB

When moral courage feels it is in the right, there is no personal daring of which it is incapable. LEIGH HUNT

Courage is fear holding on a minute longer. GEORGE S. PATTON

Bravery is fear sneering at itself. MAXWELL BODENHEIM

True courage is like a kite; a contrary wind raises it higher. J. PETIT-SENN

It is better to be the widow of a hero than the wife of a coward. DOLORES IBARRURI

Challenges

A prudent person foresees the danger
ahead and takes precautions. The
simpleton goes blindly on and suffers
the consequences.

PROVERBS 27:12

Challenges

Why can't problems hit us when we're seventeen and know everything?

Problems are only opportunities in work clothes.

HENRY J. KAISER

The best way to solve your own problem is to help someone else solve his.

If a care is too small to be turned into a prayer, it is too small to be made into a burden.

So you've got a problem? That's good! Why? Because repeated victories over your problems are the rungs on your ladder to success. With each victory you grow in wisdom, stature and experience. You become a bigger, better, more successful person each time you meet a problem and tackle and conquer it with a positive mental attitude.

CLEMENT STONE

Congress has figured out the right system. When its members encounter a problem they can't solve, they subsidize it.

A harried housewife in Omaha sighed, "I have so many problems that if something terrible happened to me it would be at least two weeks before I could get around to worrying about it."

Part of the problem today is that we have a surplus of simple answers and a shortage of simple questions.

The right angle for approaching a difficult problem is the "try-angle."

The challenge the average housekeeper faces is that she has too much month left over at the end of the money.

Children

The father of godly children has cause
for joy. What a pleasure it is to have
wise children. So give your parents joy!
May she who gave you birth be happy.

PROVERBS 23:24-25

Even children are known by the way
they act, whether their conduct is pure
and right. Children who mistreat their
father or chase away their mother are
a public disgrace and
an embarrassment.

PROVERBS 20:11; 19:26

Teach your children to choose the right
path, and when they are older, they will
remain upon it.

PROVERBS 22:6

Children

A man is never so tall as when he stoops to help a child.

A child, like your stomach, doesn't need all you can afford to give.
                                                    FRANK A. CLARK

The best way to keep children at home is to make the home atmosphere pleasant—and let the air out of the tires.
                                                    DOROTHY PARKER

If children grew up according to early indications, we should have nothing but geniuses.
                                                    GOETHE

The child who is being raised strictly by the book is probably a first edition.

We are all geniuses up to the age of ten.
                                                    ALDOUS HUXLEY

Small children give you headache; big children, heartache.

When you give a small child his first hammer, the whole world becomes a nail.

Have you ever wondered why the sounds of the words *chocolate pudding* carry farther through the air than the words *pick up your toys?*

Did you hear about the mother who says her children are miniatures because the miniature back is turned they're in trouble?

Having children is like having a bowling alley installed in your brain.
                                                    MARTIN MULL

A boy is an appetite with the skin pulled over it.

Childhood is that wonderful time of life when all you have to do to lose weight is take a bath.

The hardest job kids face today is learning good manners without seeing any. FRED ASTAIRE

Children today are tyrants. They contradict their parents, gobble their food, and tyrannize their teachers. SOCRATES

The persons hardest to convince that they are at the retirement age are children at bedtime.

Children are like mosquitoes: the minute they stop making a noise, you know they're getting into something.

Many a spoiled child is the kind of youngster his mother tells him not to play with.

A child only educated at school is an uneducated child. GEORGE SANTAYANA

It's not easy to be crafty and winsome at the same time, and few accomplish it after the age of six. DAVID SUTTEN

Now that we have perfected guided missiles, the only things left that need guidance are our children.

It's clear that most children suffer too much mother and too little father. GLORIA STEINEM

Children are growing up when they start asking questions parents can answer.

It's amazing how sophisticated kids have become. Two six-year-olds were talking. One said, "Let's play doctor. You operate. I'll sue!"

Children who are seen and not heard have just done something awful.

One thing children save for a rainy day is lots of energy.

The easiest children to bring up are calm, thoughtful—and belong to someone else.

There's nothing thirstier than a child who has just gone to bed.

The reason some parents want their children to play the piano instead of the violin is that it's harder to lose a piano.

Children may be deductible, but they're still taxing.

The secret of dealing successfully with a child is not to be its parent.   MELL LAZARUS

If you don't have any children, what do you do for aggravation?   CAROL CRANE

Raising children is as difficult as nailing poached eggs to a tree.

God made children cute so they could be tolerated until they get some sense.

I can handle any crisis; I have children.

When a teacher calls a boy by his entire name, it means trouble.   MARK TWAIN

Anything parents have not learned from experience, they can now learn from their children.

Child care: Let us care for your child. Fenced yard, meals and smacks included.

Children have more need of models than of critics.
JOSEPH JOUBERT

The well-mannered child is its parents' best advertisement.
MERIDITH NICHOLSON

A child is a thing that stands between an adult and a television set.

One of the hardest things to teach a child is that the truth is more important than the consequences.   O. A. BATTISTA

Sign on church bulletin board: Be the soul support of your children.

Nowadays, parents take a problem child to a psychiatrist. Grandfather used to keep a do-it-yourself in the woodshed.

Children, like canoes, are more easily controlled if paddled from the rear.

Choice

We can make our plans, but the Lord determines our steps.

PROVERBS 16:9

Choose a good reputation over great riches, for being held in high esteem is better than having silver or gold.

PROVERBS 22:1

Choose today whom you will serve.

JOSHUA 24:15

A double minded man is unstable in all his ways.

JAMES 1:8, KJV

Choice

There is a time when we must firmly choose the course we will follow, or the relentless drift of events will make the decision.   HERBERT V. PROCHNOW

One of life's difficult choices is picking the supermarket checkout line that will move the fastest.

Sign at the crossroads in a southwestern state: "Be careful which road you choose—you'll be on it for the next 200 miles."

No one learns to make right decisions without being free to make wrong ones.

Somewhere along the line of our development we discover what we really are, and then we make our decision for which we are responsible. Make that decision primarily for yourself because you can never live anyone else's life. ELEANOR ROOSEVELT

He who insists on seeing with perfect clearness before he decides never decides.   HENRI FREDERIC AMIEL

"I see what's wrong," whispered the referee to himself, as threats and nasty remarks were coming from every direction for his last decision. "The ref should be stationed in the grandstands!"

In every success story, you find someone has made a courageous decision.   PETER F. DRUCKER

Making a decision, even a bad one, is better than making no decision at all.   JESSE AWEIDA

Your capacity to say "No" determines your capacity to say "Yes" to greater things. E. STANLEY JONES

We make our decisions, and then our decisions turn around and make us. R. W. BOREHAM

Between two evils, choose neither; between two goods, choose both. TYRON EDWARDS

We forge the chains we wear in life. CHARLES DICKENS

Most of us can, as we choose, make of this world either a palace or a prison. JOHN LUBBOCK

We live by making choices. DAVID FINK

Choice, not change, determines human destiny.

If you would achieve your goals and be a successful, dynamic person, then your very first step must be to make up your mind. ALFRED ARMAND MONTAPERT

Look at it, size it up, but don't "postpone your life" just because you can't make up your mind. OMAR BRADLEY

Decision and perseverance are the noblest qualities of man. GOETHE

Decision—what an executive is forced to make when he can't get anyone to serve on a committee.

No wind serves him who addresses his voyage to no certain port. MICHEL DE MONTAIGNE

God provides the nuts, but he does not crack them.

Procrastination is the art of keeping up with yesterday.

DON MARQUIS

A man should give a lot of thought to a sudden decision.

Regardless of circumstances, each man lives in a world of his own making.   JOSEPH MURRAY EMMS

What appears to be patience may be simply the inability to make a decision.

Choice is the strongest principle of growth.   GEORGE ELIOT

The power of choice must involve the possibility of error—that is the essence of choosing.   HERBERT L. SAMUEL

No choice is also a choice.   JEWISH PROVERB

Choice is life's business.   ROBERT BROWNING

Once the facts are clear, the decision jumps at you.

PETER F. DRUCKER

To every man is given the power of choice.

Nothing ranks a man so quickly as his skill in selecting things that are really worthwhile. Every day brings the necessity of keen discrimination. Not always is it a choice between good and bad, but between good and best.   A. P. GOUTHEY

An individual chooses and makes himself.   JEAN-PAUL SARTRE

The doors we open and close each day decide the lives we live.

FLORA WHITTEMORE

There's small choice in rotten apples.   WILLIAM SHAKESPEARE

So it is, life is actually made up of our choices. We are the sum total of them, and if we hold to an attitude of love and thanksgiving for all the good things within our grasp we may have what all ambitious people long for—success.   DELMA NEELEY

The man who has not learned to say no will be a weak and wretched man as long as he lives.

Making decisions is simple: get the facts; seek God's guidance; form a judgment; act on it; worry no more. CHARLES E. BENNETT

My only difficulty is to choose or reject.   A. P. GOUTHEY

Church

How wonderful it is, how pleasant,
when brothers live together in
harmony!

PSALM 133:1

———

A home divided against itself is
doomed.

JESUS, MARK 3:25

Church

Attend the church of your choice every Sunday and avoid the Easter rush.

When I am passing by a church
    I always stop to visit,
So that when I'm carried in
    The Lord won't say, "Who is it?"

Before church, we talk to God; during church, God talks to us; after church, we talk to our neighbors.

A nickel isn't supposed to be as good as a dollar, but it goes to church more often.

If all the people who go to sleep in church were laid end-to-end, they would be more comfortable.

A collection is a church function in which most of the people take but a passing interest.

Many people find the sermon cold because they insist on sitting in "Z" row.

Some families think that church is like a convention where you send a delegate—and it's usually Mother.

A little boy was asked what his church was, and he replied, "I'm a Seventh-Day Absentist!"

This ad appeared in a Minnesota newspaper: "Wanted: men, women and children to sit in slightly used pews Sunday morning."

If you want to know all about church trouble, just ask someone who hasn't been there for six months.

Church: a place where you encounter nodding acquaintances.

A church is not a museum, an exhibition of saints, a showring of pious purebreds. A church is a school, a group of people in various stages of development, from beginners in the Christian life with the dirt of the world still on them to those clad in the white robes of the saints.

METHODIST BISHOP F. GERALD ENSLEY

If absence really made the heart grow fonder, a lot of people would miss church more than anyplace in the world.

The church is fairly well supplied with conductors. It shows a shortage of engineers but an overload of brakemen.

A cold church is like cold butter—it never spreads very well.

What kind of a church would my church be if all of its members were just like me?

The seven last words of the church are "We never did it that way before...."

The world at its worst needs the church at its best.

Churchgoers are like coals of fire. When they cling together, they keep the flame aglow; when they separate, they die out.

BILLY GRAHAM

Too many say "Our Father" on Sunday and spend the rest of the week acting like orphans.

The church that does not evangelize will freeze or fossilize.

Often church members are like autos; they start missing before they quit.

You quickly lose interest in the church if you have nothing invested.

Floating church members cause a sinking ship.

The church is never a place but always a people; never a fold but always a flock; never a sacred building but always a believing assembly.

A minister asked a little girl what she thought of her first church service. "The music was nice," she said, "but the commercial was too long."

Quitters in the church are like motors—they sputter before they miss and miss before they quit.

"Why don't you come to my church next Sunday?" the little boy asked.
"Because I belong to another abomination," the answer came.

From church bulletins:
"Ladies, don't forget the rummage sale. It's a good chance to get rid of those things not worth keeping around the house. Bring your husbands!"

The sermon: "Gossip"
Invitation hymn: "I Love to Tell the Story"

From outdoor church signs:
"Come in, and let us prepare you for your finals."

"We specialize in faith-lifting."

"David and Bathsheba—you've seen the movie, now read the book."

"Ask about our pray-as-you-go plan."

"This church is prayer-conditioned."

"Merry Christmas to our Christian friends. Happy Hanukkah to our Jewish friends. To our atheist friends—good luck."

"What on earth are you doing for heaven's sake?"

"Church membership does not make you a Christian any more than owning a piano makes you a musician."

"Worship: the stop that keeps you going."

Committee

Plans succeed through good counsel.

PROVERBS 20:18

———

So don't go to war without wise
guidance; victory depends on having
many counselors.

PROVERBS 24:6

Committee

Outside of traffic, there is nothing that has held this country
back as much as committees. WILL ROGERS

Committee: a group of men who individually can do nothing
but as a group decide nothing can be done. FRED ALLEN

To kill time, a committee is the perfect weapon.
LAURENCE J. PETER

God so loved the world that he did not send a committee.

If Moses had been a committee, the Israelites would still be in
Egypt. J. B. HUGHES

Camel: a horse that was designed by a committee.

Search all the parks
In all of your cities . . .
You'll find no monuments
To any committees.

If Columbus had had an Advisory Committee, he would
probably still be at the dock. ARTHUR GOLDBERG

Having served on various committees, I have drawn up a list
of rules: Never arrive on time; this stamps you as a beginner.
Don't say anything until the meeting is half over; this stamps
you as being wise. Be as vague as possible; this avoids irritating
the others. When in doubt, suggest that a subcommittee be
appointed. Be the first to move for adjournment; this will
make you popular; it's what everyone is waiting for.

HARRY CHAPMAN

Common Sense

Everyone admires a person with good sense, but a warped mind is despised.

PROVERBS 12:8

———

A person with good sense is respected; a treacherous person walks a rocky road.

PROVERBS 13:15

———

Getting wisdom is the most important thing you can do! And whatever else you do, get good judgment.

PROVERBS 4:7

Common Sense

A little common sense would prevent most divorces—and marriages, too.

Horse sense is what keeps a woman from becoming a nag.

A handful of common sense is worth a bushel of learning.

SPANISH PROVERB

The ideal combination in traffic is to have the horse sense of the driver equal the horsepower of the car.

Emotion makes the world go round, but common sense keeps it from going too fast.

An unusual amount of common sense is something called wisdom.

Complaining

Don't grumble about each other, my
brothers and sisters, or God will judge
you. For look! The great Judge is
coming. He is standing at the door!

JAMES 5:9

In everything you do, stay away from
complaining and arguing, so that
no one can speak a word of
blame against you.

PHILIPPIANS 2:14-15

Complaining

Customer: "Do you sell dog biscuits in this rotten little shop?"
Clerk: "Yessir, would you like to eat them here, or shall I send them to your kennel?"

Boss to employee: "Of course my door is always open, Adam! But it's for fresh air—not complaints."

Those individuals who always are quick
   With specific complaints that they're citing,
Will back off immediately when they are asked
   To please submit them in writing.   ERICA H. STUX

Sweep the snow from your own front door before you complain about the frost on your neighbor's tiles.

Two women were heard conversing over the back fence.
"My," said one, "isn't this a beautiful day?"
"Yes," said the other, "but it's raining somewhere."

Sign over a rack of umbrellas: "Don't frown at the rain; it's the only thing coming down."

Complaint window: Fast feuds counter.   DAISY BROWN

"Whines" are the products of sour grapes.

A man who sits in a swamp all day waiting to shoot a duck will kick if his wife has dinner ten minutes late.

If you can't be grateful for what you receive, be grateful for what you escape.

He who forgets the language of gratitude can never be on speaking terms with happiness.

Conscience

The Lord's searchlight penetrates
the human spirit, exposing
every hidden motive.

PROVERBS 20:27

———

Brothers, I have always lived before
God in all good conscience!

THE APOSTLE PAUL, ACTS 23:1

Conscience

Conscience: something that feels terrible when everything else feels wonderful.

Conscience is God's presence in man.   EMANUEL SWEDENBORG

Conscience is a device that doesn't keep you from doing anything; it just keeps you from enjoying it.

When a man won't listen to his conscience, it's usually because he doesn't want advice from a stranger.

And I know of the future judgment
    How dreadful so'er it be
That to sit alone with my conscience
    Would be judgment enough for me.   CHARLES STUBBS

Many people have their bad memory to thank for their clear conscience.

Conscience is a playback of the still small voice that told you not to do it in the first place.

Labor to keep alive in your breast that little spark of celestial fire called conscience.   GEORGE WASHINGTON

Conscience is that inner voice that warns us someone is watching.

Conscience is the root of all true courage; if a man would be brave, let him obey his conscience.   J. F. CLARKE

The line is often too busy when the conscience wishes to speak.

Quite often when a man thinks his mind is getting broader, it's only his conscience stretching.

A guilty conscience is the mother of invention. CAROLYN WELLS

He who has a fight with his conscience and loses, wins.

A man's conscience takes up more room than all the rest of his insides. HUCK FINN

There is no hell like a bad conscience. JOHN CROWNE

A conscience is what makes you feel guilty for doing what it wasn't strong enough to keep you from doing.

Small boy's definition of conscience: something that makes you tell your mother before your sister does.

The conscience is a built-in feature
    That haunts the sinner, helps the preacher.
Some sins it makes us turn and run from,
    But most it simply takes the fun from. RICHARD ARMOUR

The world would be better off if people paid as much attention to their consciences as they do to their neighbors' opinions.

A man has less conscience when in love than in any other condition. SCHOPENHAUER

Conscience is that small inner voice that tells you the IRS might check your return.

Conscience helps, but the fear of getting caught doesn't do any harm either.

The nagging conscience learns to live with the evils it cannot cure. GEORGE THOMSON

Conscience, like a pencil, needs to be sharpened occasionally.

Your conscience is what your mother told you before you were six months old. G. B. CHISHOLM

Living with a conscience is like driving a car with the brakes on. BUDD SCHULBERG

Conscience gets a lot of credit that belongs to cold feet.

Conscience, a terrifying little spite that bat-like winks by day and wakes by night. JOHN WOLCOT

Conscience is like a baby; it has to go to sleep before you do.

It is neither safe nor prudent to do anything against the conscience. MARTIN LUTHER

The testimony of a good conscience is worth more than a dozen character witnesses.

Conscience is that still small voice that yells so loud the morning after.

There is only one way to achieve happiness on this terrestrial ball, and that is to have a clear conscience or none at all. OGDEN NASH

A statesman is a person who takes his ear from the ground and listens to the still small voice.

What better bed than conscience good, to pass the night in sleep. THOMAS TUSSER

The man who loses his conscience has nothing left that is
worth keeping.   IZAAK WALTON

There is no substitute for conscience. Unless, of course, it's
witnesses.   FRANKLIN P. JONES

There is no better tranquilizer than a clear conscience.

Control

A fool gives full vent to anger, but a
wise person quietly holds it back.

PROVERBS 29:11

Those who control their anger have
great understanding; those with a
hasty temper will make mistakes.

PROVERBS 14:29

Those who control their tongue will
have a long life; a quick retort
can ruin everything.

PROVERBS 13:3

It is better to be patient than
powerful; it is better to have
self-control than to conquer a city.

PROVERBS 16:32

Control

To stay out of hot water, keep a cool head.

Control your thoughts; they may break into words at any time.

He who talks without thinking runs more risks than he who thinks without talking.

I never preach religion to my players, but I won't tolerate profanity. This isn't for moral reasons. Profanity to me symbolizes loss of control; self-discipline is absolutely necessary to winning basketball.　　COACH JOHN WOODEN

A man's conquest of himself dwarfs the ascent of Everest.
ELI J. SCHIEFER

He who thinks twice before saying nothing is wise.

He who lives without self-control is exposed to grievous ruin.

Poise is the act of raising your eyebrows instead of the roof.

Those who wish to transform the world must be able to transform themselves.　　KONRAD HEIDEN

But I will write of him who fights
    And vanquishes his sins,
Who struggles on through weary years
    Against himself and wins.　　CAROLINE BEGELOW LEROW

If a man keeps his trap shut, the world will beat a path to his door.

You can't control the length of your life, but you can control its width and depth. You can't control the contour of your face, but you can control its expression. You can't control the weather, but you can control the atmosphere of your mind. Why worry about things you can't control when you can keep yourself busy controlling the things that depend on you?

Self-control is coolness and absence of heat and waste.

RALPH WALDO EMERSON

He that would govern others, first should be the master of himself.

Remember that there is always a limit to self-indulgence, but none to self-restraint.   M. K. GANDHI

The emptier the pot, the quicker the boil—watch your temper!

Character does not reach its best until it is controlled, harnessed, and disciplined.

A diplomat can keep his shirt on while getting something off his chest.

The best executive is the one who has sense enough to pick good people to do what he wants done and self-restraint enough to keep from meddling with them while they do it.

Self-control is giving up smoking cigarettes; extreme self-control is not telling anyone about it.

Have you ever noticed that control comes in mighty handy when you're eating salted peanuts?

Women in supermarkets should exercise shelf-control.

Counsel

Pay attention and grow wise, for I
am giving you good guidance. Don't
turn away from my teaching.

PROVERBS 4:1-2

———

I will teach you wisdom's ways and
lead you in straight paths. If you live
a life guided by wisdom, you won't
limp or stumble as you run.

PROVERBS 4:11-12

———

Get all the advice and instruction you
can, and be wise the rest of your life.

PROVERBS 19:20

———

Timely advice is as lovely as
golden apples in a silver basket.

PROVERBS 25:11

Counsel

The reason God made woman last was that he didn't want any advice while creating man.

Give neither counsel nor salt until you are asked for it.
ARABIC PROVERB

Raised voices lower esteem. Hot tempers cool friendships. Loose tongues stretch truth. Swelled heads shrink influence. Sharp words dull respect.   WILLIAM A. WARD

Guidance means that I can count on God; commitment means that God can count on me.

Advice is what we ask for when we already know the answer but wish we didn't.   ERICA MANN YONG

Don't be discouraged if your children reject your advice. Years later they will offer it to their own offspring.

Advising a fool is like beating the air with a stick.

The boss looks on me as a sort of consultant; he told me when he wants my advice, he'll ask for it.

The way to be successful is to follow the advice you give to others.

A theology major came to Charles Spurgeon one day, greatly concerned that he could not grasp the meaning of certain Bible verses. The noted preacher replied kindly but firmly, "Young man, allow me to give you this word of advice. Give the Lord credit for knowing things you don't understand."

To profit from good advice requires more wisdom than to give it.

Advice is one thing most people would rather give than get.

A *Father's Advice*
Sending his son out into the world, a father gave him the following rules, without which he said he could not hope to get on:

> Tell the truth—falsehoods are hard to remember.
> Shine the heels of your shoes as well as the toes.
> Don't lend money to your friends—you will lose both.
> Don't watch the clock; it will keep on going—you do the same.
> You do not need clean cuffs every day, but you need a clean conscience all the time.
> Don't borrow money, unless you positively have the wherewithal to pay it back—and then you don't need it.

Any man who has to ask for advice probably isn't married.

It's a pleasure to give advice, humiliating to need it, normal to ignore it.

No one gives advice with more enthusiasm than an ignorant person.

Advice is like snow—the softer it falls, the deeper it goes.

"Be yourself" is about the worst advice you can give to some people.

A pint of example is worth a gallon of advice.

Criticism

If you ignore criticism, you will end in poverty and disgrace; if you accept criticism, you will be honored.

PROVERBS 13:18

If you listen to constructive criticism, you will be at home among the wise. If you reject criticism, you only harm yourself; but if you listen to correction, you grow in understanding.

PROVERBS 15:31-32

Don't speak evil against each other, my dear brothers and sisters. If you criticize each other and condemn each other, then you are criticizing and condemning God's law.

JAMES 4:11

Criticism

He who constantly criticizes his inferiors hasn't any.

You'll never move up if you are continually running somebody down.

He who blows out the other fellow's candle won't make his own shine any brighter.

Critics are people who go places and boo things.

Have you ever noticed that most knocking is done by folks who don't know how to ring the bell?

He who cannot stand the heat should stay out of the kitchen.

HARRY TRUMAN

If you're not big enough to stand criticism, you're too small to be praised.

He who throws dirt loses ground.

Handling criticism: if it's untrue, disregard it; if it's unfair, keep from irritation; if it's ignorant, smile; if it's justified, learn from it.

He has the right to criticize who has the heart to help.

ABRAHAM LINCOLN

Criticism should not be querulous and wasting, all knife and root-pulling, but guiding, instructive, inspirational—a south wind and not an east wind.

RALPH WALDO EMERSON

Death and Life

Godly people find life;
evil people find death.

PROVERBS 11:19

―――

The way of the godly leads to life;
their path does not lead to death.

PROVERBS 12:28

―――

For whoever finds me [wisdom] finds
life and wins approval from the Lord.
But those who miss me have injured
themselves. All who hate me love
death.

PROVERBS 8:35-36

Death and Life

There is a tide in the affairs of men
Which taken at the flood, leads on to fortune;
Omitted, all the voyage of their life,
Is bound in shallows and in miseries.   WILLIAM SHAKESPEARE

Life can only be understood backward; it must be lived
forward.   SØREN KIERKEGAARD

Life is what happens while you're making other plans.

Life is fragile; handle with prayer.

I'm not afraid to die. I just don't want to be there when it
happens.   WOODY ALLEN

I hate death; in fact, I could live forever without it.   POGO

Man looking at the obituaries: "Strange, isn't it, how everyone
seems to die in alphabetical order?"

Not only does life begin at forty—it begins to show.

The first half of our life is ruined by our parents and the
second half by our children.   CLARENCE DARROW

The trouble with life is that it is so daily.

Live each day as if it were your last—someday you'll be right.

He who lives to live forever, never fears dying.   WILLIAM PENN

A life of ease is a difficult pursuit.   WILLIAM COWPER

The clock of life is wound but once,
And no man has the power
To tell when the hands will stop,
At late or early hour.

Now is the only time you own;
Live, love, work with a will.
Place no faith in tomorrow;
The clock may then be still.

It wasn't until quite late in life that I discovered how easy it
was to say, "I don't know."   W. SOMERSET MAUGHAM

As a well-spent day brings happy sleep, so a life well spent
brings happy death.   LEONARDO DA VINCI

Life's race well run,
Life's work well done,
Life's victory won,
Now cometh rest.   E. H. PARKER

The greatest use of life is to spend it for something that
outlasts it.   WILLIAM JAMES

My Task

To love someone more dearly every day,
To help a wandering child to find his way,
To ponder o'er a noble thought, and pray,
And smile when evening falls.
This is my task.

To follow truth as blind men long for light,
To do my best from dawn of day till night,
To keep my heart fit for His holy sight,
And answer when He calls.
This is my task.   MAUDE LOUISE RAY

Life is my university, and I hope to graduate from it with some distinction. LOUISA MAY ALCOTT

The awful importance of this life is that it determines eternity. WILLIAM BARCLAY

Your life is like a coin. You can spend it any way you wish, but you can spend it only once. LILLIAN DICKSON

I affirm life; I challenge problems; I accept responsibility; I believe in God; I live today. ELIZABETH SEARLE LAMB

It is we ourselves and not outward circumstances who make death what it can be, a death freely and voluntarily accepted. DIETRICH BONHOEFFER

Ninety-five percent of the people who died today had expected to live a lot longer. ALBERT M. WELLS JR.

The Christian does not consider death to be the end of his life, but the end of his troubles. A. MARK WELLS

So live, that when thy summons comes to join
The innumerable caravan which moves
To the mysterious realm, where each shall take
His chamber in the silent halls of death,
Thou go not, like the quarry-slave at night,
Scourged to his dungeon, but, sustained and soothed
Like one who wraps the drapery of his couch
About him, and lies down to pleasant dreams.
WILLIAM CULLEN BRYANT

The hardest thing of all—to die rightly—an exam nobody is spared—and how many pass it? DAG HAMMARSKJÖLD

We make a living by what we get—a life by what we give.

Death is not a period
Bringing the sentence of life to a close
Like the spilling of a moment
Or the dissolution of an hour.

Death is a useful comma
Which punctuates, and labors
To convince
Of much to follow.   JOHN DONNE

Defeat

Pride goes before destruction, and
haughtiness before a fall.

PROVERBS 16:18

Defeat

The road to defeat is greased with the slime of indifference.

Defeat isn't bitter if you don't swallow it.

Show me a man who is a good loser and I'll show you a man who is playing golf with his boss.

Defeat never comes to any man until he admits it.
JOSEPH DANIELS

After resigning as coach of the Iowa State women's basketball team, which finished the season with fourteen straight defeats, Lynn Wheeler remarked: "I've taken this team as far as I can."

He who leaves home to set the world on fire often comes back for more matches.

The only thing you get for nothing is failure.

A college freshman phoned home saying, "Mom, I've failed everything. Prepare Pop!"
The next day Mom replied, "Pop prepared. Prepare yourself!"

Ninety-nine percent of defeats come from people who have the habit of making excuses.

The man who wins may have been counted out several times, but he didn't hear the referee.
H. E. JANSEN

"How did your horse happen to win the race?" the visitor asked the jockey.
"Well, I just kept whispering in his ear," replied the jockey. "Roses are red, violets are blue—horses that lose are made into glue."

Determination

They may trip seven times, but each
time they will rise again.
But one calamity is enough
to lay the wicked low.

PROVERBS 24:16

———

Good planning and hard work lead
to prosperity, but hasty shortcuts lead
to poverty.

PROVERBS 21:5

Determination

Nothing is so common as unsuccessful men with talent. They lack only determination. CHARLES SWINDOLL

Some men succeed because they are destined to, but most men because they are determined to.

He who doesn't climb the mountain cannot see the view.

Personnel manager to applicant: "What we're after is a man of vision; a man with drive, determination, fire; a man who never quits; a man who can inspire others; a man who can pull the company's bowling team out of last place!"

A dead fish can float downstream, but it takes a live fish to swim upstream.

I am only one, but I am one. I cannot do everything, but I can do something; and what I can do, that I ought to do; and what I ought to do, by the grace of God I shall do.

EDWARD EVERETT HALE

Big shots are only little shots who kept on shooting.

DALE CARNEGIE

Curious people ask questions; determined people find answers.

Consider the hammer: It keeps its head. It doesn't fly off the handle. It keeps pounding away. It finds the point, then drives it home. It looks at the other side, too, and thus clinches the matter. It makes mistakes, but when it does, it starts all over.

The difference between an unsuccessful person and others is not a lack of strength, not a lack of knowledge, but rather a lack of will.

VINCE LOMBARDI

Direction

Seek his will in all you do,
and he will direct your paths.

PROVERBS 3:6

———

How can we understand the road we
travel? It is the Lord who directs
our steps.

PROVERBS 20:24

Direction

The winds of God are always blowing, but you must set the sails.

He who takes the wrong direction has a long road ahead.

The world stands aside to let anyone pass who knows where he is going.   DAVID STAFF JORDAN

The greatest thing in the world is not so much where we are, but in what direction we are moving.   OLIVER WENDELL HOLMES

It is comforting to know that not only the *steps* but also the *stops* of a good man are ordered by the Lord.   GEORGE MUELLER

It isn't enough to make sure you're on the right track; you must also make sure you're going in the right direction.

When success turns a man's head, it always leaves him facing in the wrong direction.

When a woman says she's approaching middle age, she never tells you from which direction.

Paying as you go is all right, but first make sure you're going in the right direction.

Discipline

For a servant, mere words are not
enough—discipline is needed.
For the words may be understood,
but they are not heeded.

PROVERBS 29:19

———

To discipline and reprimand a child
produces wisdom, but a mother is
disgraced by an undisciplined child.

PROVERBS 29:15

———

If you love your children, you will be
prompt to discipline them.

PROVERBS 13:24

Discipline

Discipline is the refining fire by which talent becomes ability.

No pain, no palm; no thorns, no throne; no gall, no glory;
no cross, no crown.   WILLIAM PENN

The undisciplined man is a headache to himself and a
heartache to others and is unprepared to face the stern
realities of life.

Discipline, once considered "standard household equipment,"
has fallen on hard times, and in its place permissiveness
reigns.

Discipline: shorten his reign.

Draw your salary before spending it.   GEORGE ADE

He who lives without discipline is exposed to grievous ruin.
                                            THOMAS À KEMPIS

A lot of us can recall when a wayward child was straightened
up by being bent over.

The cure for crime is not in the *electric* chair but in the *high*
chair.

Storms make oaks take deeper root.   GEORGE SANTAYANA

One reason for juvenile delinquency: parents don't burn their
kids' britches behind them.

Discipline yourself so others won't need to.

Dreams

God . . . is able to do far more than we
would dare to ask or even dream
of—infinitely beyond our highest
prayers, desires, thoughts or hopes.

EPHESIANS 3:20, TLB

Dreams

Some people who think they are dreamers are just sleepers.

Reach high, for stars lie hidden in your soul.
Dream deep, for every dream precedes the goal.

PAMELA VAULL STARR

Some men see things as they are and say, "Why?" I dream
things that never were and say, "Why not?"

GEORGE BERNARD SHAW

It doesn't do any harm to dream, as long as you get up and
hustle when the alarm goes off.

Ah, great it is to believe the dream
    As we stand in youth by the starry stream;
But a greater thing is to fight life through,
    And at the end, "The dream is true!"   EDWIN MARKHAM

It's more fun building castles in the air than on the ground.

All air castles need a foundation.

Castles in the air are all right until you start moving into them.

They call it a "dream house" because it usually costs twice as
much as you dreamed it would.

I believe in America because we have great dreams—and
because we have the opportunity to make those dreams come
true.   WENDELL L. WILLKIE

You'll never make your dream come true by oversleeping.

People who are always walking on clouds leave too many things up in the air.

Daydreaming: wishcraft.   BERT MURRAY

Some people dream in technicolor—others add sound effects.

Don't be unhappy if your dreams never come true—just be thankful your nightmares don't.

The poorest of all men is not the man without a cent but the man without a dream.

To dream anything that you want to dream—that is the beauty of the human mind. To do anything you want to do—that is the strength of the human will. To trust yourself to test your limits—that is the courage to succeed.   BERNARD EDMONDS

I saw a man chasing the horizon. I shouted at him, "You'll never reach it!"
He replied, "You lie," and rushed on.

Did you hear about the man who dreamed he ate a five-pound marshmallow? When he woke up, his pillow was gone.

All big men are dreamers. They see things in the soft haze of a spring day or in the red fire of a long winter's evening. Some of us let our dreams die, but others nourish and protect them, nurse them through bad days till they bring them to sunshine and light, which always come to those who sincerely believe that their dreams will come true.   WOODROW WILSON

We create our future by what we dream today.

We cannot dream ourselves into what we could be.

Between tomorrow's dream and yesterday's regret is today's opportunity.

Some men believe in dreams—until they marry one.

No dream comes true until you wake up and go to work.

A house is made of walls and beams; a home is built with love and dreams.

Encouragement/ Discouragement

Worry weighs a person down; an encouraging word cheers a person up.

PROVERBS 12:25

———

Gentle words bring life and health; a deceitful tongue crushes the spirit.

PROVERBS 15:4

———

My child, don't ignore it when the Lord disciplines you, and don't be discouraged when he corrects you.

PROVERBS 3:11

Encouragement/Discouragement

A father said to his complaining and failing son: "Son, all you need is encouragement and a swift kick in the seat of your can'ts."

Success comes in cans; failure comes in can'ts.

Correction can help, but encouragement can help far more.

When Thomas A. Edison's desk was opened years after his death, this card was found among his papers: "When down in the mouth, remember Jonah. He came out all right."

If the devil cannot make you puffed up by pride, he will try to dampen your spirit by discouragement. It's his best tool!

When the outlook is dark,
And the in-look's discouraging,
Just try the up-look;
It's always encouraging.

Don't be discouraged; it may be the last key in the bunch that opens the door.   STONSIFER

He who eats pillows is down in the mouth.

I never allow myself to become discouraged under any circumstances. . . . The three great essentials to achieve anything worthwhile are, first, hard work; second, stick-to-itiveness; third, common sense.   THOMAS A. EDISON

Appreciation is thanking, recognition is seeing, and encouragement is bringing hope for the future.

Encouragement after censure is as the sun after a shower.

GOETHE

Don't discourage the other man's plans unless you have better ones to offer.

A smile of encouragement at the right moment may act like sunlight on a closed-up flower; it may be the turning point for a struggling life.

Enthusiasm

Cry out for insight and
understanding. Search for them as you
would for lost money or hidden
treasure.

PROVERBS 2:3-4

———

If you look for me in earnest, you will
find me when you seek me.

JEREMIAH 29:13

Enthusiasm

I have never seen a man who could do real work except under the stimulus of encouragement and enthusiasm and approval of the people for whom he is working. WILLIAM MCFEE

Nothing great was ever achieved without enthusiasm.
RALPH WALDO EMERSON

Enthusiasm is a good engine, but it needs intelligence for a driver.

The fellow who is fired with enthusiasm for his work is seldom fired by his boss.

Nothing is as contagious as enthusiasm.

The gap between enthusiasm and indifference is filled with failures.

Zeal without knowledge is fanaticism.

Enthusiasm flourishes in adversity, kindles in the hour of danger, and awakens to deeds of renown.

Spread your arms to those with needs,
    And serve with joy and zest;
Fill each day with golden deeds,
    And give your very best. WILLIAM A. WARD

Enthusiasm can achieve in one day what reasoning must work at for centuries.

An enthusiast is a fellow who feels perfectly sure of the things he is mistaken about.

Excellence

Since you excel in so many ways—you
have so much faith, such gifted
speakers, such knowledge, such
enthusiasm, and such love for
us—now I want you to excel also in
this gracious ministry of giving.

THE APOSTLE PAUL, 2 CORINTHIANS 8:7

———

Think about things that are excellent
and worthy of praise.

PHILIPPIANS 4:8

Excellence

Excellence in any art or profession is attained only by hard
and persistent work.   THEODORE MARTIN

Excellence is not a matter of chance, it's a matter of choice.

Human excellence means nothing unless it works with the
consent of God.   EURIPIDES

The quality of a person's life is in direct proportion to that
person's commitment to excellence, regardless of the chosen
field of endeavor.   VINCE LOMBARDI

Excellence is to do a common thing in an uncommon way.
                                           BOOKER T. WASHINGTON

Excellence is never granted to man but as the reward of labor.
                                           SIR JOSHUA REYNOLDS

Every job is a self-portrait of the person who did it.
Autograph your work with excellence.

A total commitment is paramount to reaching the ultimate in
performance.

The difference between failure and success is doing a thing
nearly right and doing a thing exactly right.   EDWARD SIMMONS

Some men dream of worthy accomplishments, while others
stay awake and do them.

Desire is the key to motivation, but it's the determination
and commitment to unrelenting pursuit of your goal—a
commitment to excellence—that will enable you to attain the
success you seek.   MARIO ANDRETTI

Well done is better than well said. BENJAMIN FRANKLIN

The secret of joy is contained in one word—*excellence*. To know how to do something well is to enjoy it. PEARL S. BUCK

The price of success is hard work, dedication to the job at hand, and the determination that whether we win or lose, we have applied the best of ourselves to the task at hand.
VINCE LOMBARDI

No one ever attains very eminent success by simply doing what is required of him; it is the amount of excellence of what is over and above the required, that determines the greatness of ultimate distinction. CHARLES KENDALL ADAMS

Ingenuity, plus courage, plus work equals miracles.
BOB RICHARDS

It's a funny thing about life: If you refuse to accept anything but the very best, you will often get it. W. SOMERSET MAUGHAM

There is no excellence uncoupled with difficulties. OVID

Excellence resides in quality, not in quantity. The best is always few and rare; much lowers value. GRACIAN

In character, in manner, in style, in all things, the supreme excellence is simplicity. HENRY WADSWORTH LONGFELLOW

Hit the ball over the fence and you can take your time going around the bases. JOHN W. RAPER

One of the rarest things that a man ever does is to do the best he can. JOSH BILLINGS

Experience

Once I was young, and now I am old.
Yet I have never seen the godly
forsaken, nor seen their children
begging for bread.

PSALM 37:25

The glory of the young is their
strength; the gray hair of experience is
the splendor of the old.

PROVERBS 20:29

Experience

Experience is a wonderful thing. It enables you to recognize a mistake when you make it again.

Listen to the voice of experience, but also make use of your brains.

Experience—something we would be glad to sell for less than we paid for it.

A new broom sweeps clean, but an old one knows where the dirt is.

Experience is not what happens to you, it is what you do with what happens to you.   ALDOUS HUXLEY

There's no fool like an old fool—you just can't beat experience.

We should be careful to get out of an experience only the wisdom that is in it—and stop there; lest we be like the cat that sits down on a hot stove-lid. She will never sit down on a hot stove-lid again—and that is well; but also she will never sit down on a cold one anymore.   MARK TWAIN

One thorn of experience is worth a whole wilderness of warning.

Experience is a hard teacher because she gives the test first, the lesson afterwards.   VERNON LAW

Fact

Fools have no interest in
understanding; they only want
to air their own opinions.

PROVERBS 18:2

———

"You simpletons!" she cries. "How
long will you go on being
simpleminded? How long will you
mockers relish your mocking? How
long will you fools fight the facts?"

PROVERBS 1:22

Fact

Facts do not cease to exist because they are ignored.

ALDOUS HUXLEY

Digging for facts is better mental exercise than jumping to conclusions.

Every man has a right to his opinion, but no man has a right to be wrong in his facts.   BERNARD BARUCH

The hardest thing about facts is facing them.

A hard-liner's admission: "My mind's made up! Don't confuse me with the facts!"

We wouldn't call him a liar. Let's just say that he lives on the wrong side of the facts.

Facts are stubborn things.   TOBIAS SMOLLEN

Get your facts first; then you can distort 'em as you please.

MARK TWAIN

When you shoot an arrow of truth, dip its point in honey.

ARABIC PROVERB

A sure way to stop a red-hot argument is to lay a few cold facts on it.

The people, when given the facts, will never make a mistake.

THOMAS JEFFERSON

Facts, when combined with ideas, constitute the greatest force in the world.

Family

Those who bring trouble on their families inherit only the wind. The fool will be a servant to the wise.

PROVERBS 11:29

God places the lonely in families; he sets the prisoners free and gives them joy.

PSALM 68:6

But he rescues the poor from their distress and increases their families like vast flocks of sheep.

PSALM 107:41

Family

Some families can trace their ancestry back three hundred years but can't tell you where the children were last night.

Nothing keeps a family together like having one car in the shop.

Happy families are all alike; every unhappy one is unhappy in its own way.   LEO TOLSTOY

A happy family is but an earlier heaven.   JOHN BOWRING

The presidency is temporary, but the family is permanent.
                YVONNE DE GAULLE, FORMER FIRST LADY OF FRANCE

No one but a mule denies his family.   MOROCCAN PROVERB

Every family tree produces some nuts.

The best part of some family trees is underground.

No family should attempt an auto trip if the kids outnumber the car windows.   TERESA BLOOMINGDALE

Many a family argument has been saved by the doorbell or the telephone.

What the average man wants to get out of his new car is the kids.

Children may tear up a house, but they never break up a home.

It takes a raft of money to keep a family afloat these days.

A real family man is one who looks at his new baby as an addition rather than a deduction.

Some family trees suffer from lack of pruning.

Nowadays, the family that buys together cries together.

Father/Mother

Listen, my child, to what your father
teaches you. Don't neglect your
mother's teaching. What you learn
from them will crown you with grace
and clothe you with honor.

PROVERBS 1:8-9

Sensible children bring joy to their
father; foolish children despise
their mother.

PROVERBS 15:20

Listen to your father, who gave you
life, and don't despise your mother's
experience when she is old.

PROVERBS 23:22

If you curse your father and mother,
the lamp of your life will be
snuffed out.

PROVERBS 20:20

Father/Mother

My mother was the most beautiful woman I ever saw. All I am
I owe to my mother. GEORGE WASHINGTON

Where does the family start? It starts with a young man in love
with a girl—no superior alternative has yet been found.
WINSTON CHURCHILL

Since a child at my mother's knee, I have believed in honor,
ethics and right living for its own reward. HARRY S. TRUMAN

My best training came from my father. WOODROW WILSON

My father was the dominant person in our family and in my
life. JIMMY CARTER

As a substitute father for hundreds of youths over the past
thirteen years, I've yet to encounter a young person in trouble
whose difficulty could not be traced to the lack of a strong
father image in the home. PAUL ANDERSON

While I don't minimize the vital role played by a mother, I
believe a successful family begins with her husband.
JAMES DOBSON

What a father says to his children is not heard by the world,
but it will be heard by posterity. JEAN PAUL RICHTER

There are too many fathers who tie up their hound dog at
night and let their boys run loose.

If mothers would understand that much of their importance
lies in building up the father image for the child, the children
would turn out well. SAMUEL S. LIEBOWITZ

If Nature had arranged that husbands and wives should have children alternatively, there would never be more than *three* in a family.   LAURENCE HOUSMAN

The chances are that you'll never be elected President of the country, write the great American novel, make a million dollars, stop pollution and racial conflict, or save the world. However valid it may be to work at any of these goals, there is another one of higher priority—to be an effective parent.
                                                     LANDRUM R. BOLLING

They say that man is mighty,
He governs land and sea,
He wields a mighty scepter
O'er lesser powers than he.
But a mighty power and stronger
Man from his throne has hurled:
For the hand that rocks the cradle
is the hand that rules the world.   WILLIAM WALLACE

Let every Christian father and mother understand that when the child is three years old, they have done more than half of what they will ever do for his character.

Could I turn back the time machine, I would double the attention I gave my children and go to fewer meetings.
                                                          J. D. EPPINGA

A child is not likely to find a father in God unless he finds something of God in his father.   AUSTIN L. SORENSEN

It is easier to build boys than to mend men.

Children are a poor man's wealth.   DANISH PROVERB

Flattery

In the end, people appreciate
frankness more than flattery.

PROVERBS 28:23

————

To flatter people is to lay a trap
for their feet.

PROVERBS 29:5

Flattery

Imitation is the sincerest form of flattery.

He soft-soaped her until she couldn't see for the suds.

MARY R. RINEHART

'Tis an old maxim in the schools
That flattery's the food of fools;
Yet now and then your men of wit
Will condescend to take a bit.

JONATHAN SWIFT

Flattery is soft soap—and soap is 90 percent lye.

Tell her that she's too smart to be flattered—and flattered she is.

Baloney is flattery laid on so thick it cannot be true, and blarney is flattery so thin we love it.

BISHOP FULTON J. SHEEN

Flattery is telling others exactly what they think of themselves.

When flatterers meet, the devil goes to dinner.

DANIEL DEFOE

Nothing is so great an instance of ill manners as flattery. If you flatter all the company, you please none; if you flatter only one or two, you affront all the rest.

JONATHAN SWIFT

Flattery is a sort of bad money, to which your vanity gives currency.

Flattery makes friends, and truth makes enemies.

SPANISH PROVERB

Conscience is the only mirror that doesn't flatter.

Criticism from a friend is better than flattery from an enemy.

Flattery is like chewing gum—enjoy it briefly, but don't swallow it.

Forgiveness

Don't say, "I will get even for this wrong." Wait for the Lord to handle the matter.

PROVERBS 20:22

But when you are praying, first forgive anyone you are holding a grudge against, so that your Father in heaven will forgive your sins, too.

JESUS, MARK 11:25

Stop judging others, and you will not be judged. Stop criticizing others, or it will all come back on you. If you forgive others, you will be forgiven.

JESUS, LUKE 6:37

Be kind to each other, tenderhearted, forgiving one another, just as God through Christ has forgiven you.

EPHESIANS 4:32

Forgiveness

It is far better to forgive and forget than to hate and remember.

Always forgive your enemies; nothing annoys them quite so much.

"I can forgive, but I cannot forget," is only another way of saying, "I will not forgive." HENRY WARD BEECHER

When a friend makes a mistake, don't rub it in. Rub it out.

He who cannot forgive breaks the bridge over which he himself must pass. GEORGE HERBERT

If His conditions are met, God is bound by His Word to forgive any man or any woman of any sin because of Christ. BILLY GRAHAM

Forgiving those who hurt us is the key to personal peace. G. WEATHERLY

It isn't necessary to put a marker at the grave when we forgive and bury the hatchet.

Forgive your enemies—if you can't get back at them any other way!

A Christian will find it cheaper to pardon than to resent. Forgiveness saves the expense of anger, the cost of hatred, the waste of spirits. HANNAH MORE

Never does the human soul appear so strong and noble as when it foregoes revenge and dares to forgive an injury. E. H. CHAPIN

The kindest people are those who forgive and forget.

Friends

A friend is always loyal, and a brother
is born to help in time of need.

PROVERBS 17:17

——

A troublemaker plants seeds of strife;
gossip separates the best of friends.

PROVERBS 16:28

Friends

The best way to keep your friends is not to give them away.

Be slow to fall into friendship, but when thou art in, continue firm and constant. SOCRATES

There are good ships, and there are bad ships, but the best ships are friendships.

Three things we can all do today;
To pause a moment just to pray,
To be a friend both tried and true
And find some good that we can do. WILLIAM A. WARD

Those who bring sunshine to the lives of others cannot keep it from themselves.

Money can't buy friends, but it will buy a better class of enemies.

Look around today and share a cheerful, friendly smile; show the world you truly care, then go the second mile.
WILLIAM A. WARD

My best friend is the one who brings out the best in me.
HENRY FORD

A real friend is one who will tell you of your faults and follies in prosperity and assist with his hand and heart in adversity.

The trouble with being a grouch is that you have to make new friends every few months.

Future

Look straight ahead, and fix your eyes
on what lies before you. Mark out a
straight path for your feet; then stick
to the path and stay safe. Don't get
sidetracked; keep your feet from
following evil.

PROVERBS 4:25-27

―――

Do not fret because of evildoers;
don't envy the wicked. For the evil
have no future; their light will be
snuffed out.

PROVERBS 24:19-20

―――

Always continue to fear the Lord. For
surely you have a future ahead of you;
your hope will not be disappointed.

PROVERBS 23:17-18

Future

The future is history to God, for he is omniscient.

He who provides for this life, but takes no care for eternity, is wise for a moment, but a fool forever.   JOHN TILLOTSON

Perhaps the best thing about the future is that it comes just one day at a time.

I've Found Today
I've shut the door on Yesterday,
    Its sorrows and mistakes;
I've locked within its gloomy walls
    Past failures and heartaches.
And now I throw the key away
    To seek another room,
And furnish it with hope and smiles
    And every springtime bloom.

No thought shall enter this abode
    That has a hint of pain,
And worry, malice and distrust
    Shall never therein reign.
I've shut the door on Yesterday
    And thrown the key away—
The Future holds no doubt for me,
    Since I have found Today.   AUTHOR UNKNOWN

There is nothing like a dream to create the future.   VICTOR HUGO

The trouble with our times is that the future is not what it used to be.   PAUL VALERY

If we open a quarrel between the past and the present, we shall find that we have lost the future.   WINSTON CHURCHILL

Generosity

The desires of lazy people will be their
ruin, for their hands refuse to work.
They are always greedy for more,
while the godly love to give!

PROVERBS 21:25-26

It is possible to give freely and
become more wealthy, but those who
are stingy will lose everything. The
generous prosper and are satisfied.

PROVERBS 11:24-25

Blessed are those who are generous,
because they feed the poor.

PROVERBS 22:9

Generosity

First, give yourself to God; he can do more with you than you can.

A small gift is better than a great promise.   GERMAN PROVERB

He doubles his gift who gives it in time.

What you are is God's gift to you; what you make of yourself is your gift to God.

The wise man does not lay up treasures. The more he gives, the more he has.   CHINESE PROVERB

The essence of generosity is self-sacrifice.

He who gives to me teaches me to give.   DUTCH PROVERB

Philanthropy, like charity, must begin at home.   CHARLES LAMB

The finest gift a man can give to his age and time is the gift of a constructive and creative life.   WILFERD PETERSON

Liberality consists less in giving a great deal than in gifts well-timed.   JEAN DE LA BRUYÉRE

A rejected opportunity to give is a lost opportunity to receive.

You can give without loving, but you cannot love without giving.   AMY CARMICHAEL

It is better to give an inexpensive gift with a smile than an expensive one with a frown.

Patrick Henry shouted, "Give me liberty or give me death!" The next generation shouted, "Give me liberty!" The Now Generation shouts, "Give me!"

Some give their mite, some give with all their might, and some don't give who might.

Give to the world the best you have, and the best will come back to you. ELLA WHEELER WILCOX

No person has ever been honored for what he has received; always, for what he has given.

Little is much when God is in it.

Goals

My child, don't lose sight of good planning and insight. Hang on to them, for they fill you with life and bring you honor and respect.

PROVERBS 3:21-22

Sensible people keep their eyes glued on wisdom, but a fool's eyes wander to the ends of the earth.

PROVERBS 17:24

So I run straight to the goal with purpose in every step. I am not like a boxer who misses his punches.

THE APOSTLE PAUL, 1 CORINTHIANS 9:26

Goals

A teenager complained to a friend: "My dad wants me to have all the things he never had when he was a boy—including five straight A's on my report card."

The poor man is not he who is without a cent, but he who is without a dream.   HARRY KEMP

Choose a goal for which you are willing to exchange a piece of your life.

Aim for the top. There is plenty of room there. There are so few at the top, it's almost lonely.   SAMUEL INSULL

Climb high, climb far;
your aim the sky, your goal the star.

A person who is going nowhere can be sure of reaching his destination.

Obstacles are those frightful things you see when you take your eyes off the goal.   HANNAH MOORE

Most of us serve our ideals by fits and starts. The person who makes a success of living is the one who sees his goal steadily and aims for it unswervingly.   CECIL B. DeMILLE

Our ideals are too often like an antique chair—nice to talk about and show off but too fragile to use.

Gossip

Scoundrels hunt for scandal; their words are a destructive blaze. A troublemaker plants seeds of strife; gossip separates the best of friends.

PROVERBS 16:27-28

A gossip tells secrets, so don't hang around with someone who talks too much.

PROVERBS 20:19

Fire goes out for lack of fuel, and quarrels disappear when gossip stops.

PROVERBS 26:20

Gossip

Not everyone repeats gossip. Some improve it.

Franklin P. Jones

If you don't see it with your eyes, don't invent it with your mouth.

Scandal is gossip related by a small bore.   Elbert Hubbard

Scandal is the mud we throw.   James Russell Lowell

Gossip is winding up your tongue and letting it go.

Gossip is social sewage.   George Meredith

Gossipers turn an earful into a mouthful.

George Bernard Shaw

Gossip is what some invent and others enlarge. Jonathan Swift

Running people down is a bad habit, whether you are a gossip or a motorist.

Unless you are able to overlook idle gossip you will always be busy with unnecessary trouble.   Roy L. Smith

Plant a little gossip, and you will reap a harvest of regret.

A tongue three inches long can ruin a man six feet tall.

A dog is loved by old and young; he wags his tail and not his tongue.

Gossip always seems to travel fastest over grapevines that are slightly sour.

A gossip is a person with a keen sense of rumor.

A groundless rumor often covers a lot of ground.

Too many people spend too much time lighting the scandal-abra.

Grandparents/
Grandchildren

Good people leave an inheritance to
their grandchildren, but the sinner's
wealth passes to the godly.

PROVERBS 13:22

Grandchildren are the crowning glory
of the aged; parents are the pride of
their children.

PROVERBS 17:6

Grandparents/Grandchildren

The simplest toy, on which even the youngest child can operate, is called a grandparent. SAM LEVENSON

Admission: My life was organized until I became a grandparent.

The grandparents' job is to give their grandchildren roots and wings.

A grandparent must recognize the value of generational continuity.

What's done to children, they will do to society.
DR. KARL MENNINGER

Nothing is harder on a grandparent than watching a grandchild being corrected.

Nobody can do for little children what grandparents can do. Grandparents sort of sprinkle dust over the lives of little children. ALEX HALEY

Grandmas don't have to do anything—just be there.

A grandfather is a man-grandmother.

What Is a Grandmother? (Written by a ninety-four-year-old)

My hair is white and I'm almost blind.
The days of my youth are far behind.
My neck is stiff, can't turn my head,
And I really listen to hear what's said.

My legs are wobbly, can't hardly walk,
But, glory be, I sure can talk!
And this is the message I want you to get,
I can still get around—and I ain't dead yet!

If Mother says no, ask Grandmother.

My grandmother actually smells like a cookie and that's
enough to get any child's attention.   LEE BAILEY

Some of our modern grandparents are so young and spry that
they help Boy Scouts across the street.

No cowboy was ever faster on the draw than a grandparent
pulling a baby picture out of a wallet.

Her: "Have I told you about my grandchildren?"
Him: "No, and I thank you very much!"

Did you hear about the grandparents who were so tickled that
their grandchildren were coming to visit for a week that they
put an extra five dollars in the offering plate at church? When
the grandchildren went home at the end of the week, the
grandparents' joy must have doubled because that Sunday
they put a ten-dollar bill in the plate.

Being grandparents is God's reward for growing old.

God couldn't be everywhere, so he invented grandparents.

Grandparents: the people to take the baby to for an overmauling.

I don't know who my grandfather was; I am concerned to
know what his grandson will be.   ABRAHAM LINCOLN

A grandparent: a grandchild's press secretary.

I've seen the lights of Paris,
I've seen the lights of Rome,
But the greatest lights I've seen so far
Are the taillights on my children's car
Taking my grandkids home.

There's only one perfect grandchild in the world, and every grandparent has it.

Grandparent: a baby-sitter who doesn't hang around the refrigerator.

Grandparents are parents who have a second chance.

Just about the time she thinks her work is done, a mother becomes a grandmother.

Happiness

The godly can look forward to
happiness, while the wicked can expect
only wrath.

PROVERBS 11:23

———

Wisdom is a tree of life to those who
embrace her; happy are those who
hold her tightly.

PROVERBS 3:18

Happiness

Happiness is the delicate balance of what one is and what one has.   F. H. DENISON

Happiness is not a station to arrive at, but a manner of traveling.   MARGARET LEE RUNBECK

Happy is the housewife who sees the rainbows, not the dishes, in the soapsuds.

Bride's father to the groom: "My boy, you're the second happiest man in the world."

Happiness is the inner joy that can be sought or caught, but never taught or bought.

Happiness is hiring a baby-sitter who's on a diet.

One man's admission: "I'm happy to live in a free country where a man can do whatever his wife pleases."

The surest way to happiness is to lose yourself in a cause greater than yourself.

Happiness is making a bouquet of those flowers within reach.

The U.S. Constitution doesn't guarantee happiness, only the pursuit of it. You have to catch up to it yourself.
                                                           BENJAMIN FRANKLIN

In the pursuit of happiness, the difficulty lies in knowing when you have caught up.   R. H. GRENVILLE

Happiness is a thing to be practiced, like the violin.
                                                           JOHN LUBBOCK

It's never too late to have a happy childhood.

People don't notice whether it's summer or winter when they're happy. ANTON CHEKHOV

Happiness is the result of being too busy to be miserable.

Happiness is the smell of bread baking.

All our guests bring us happiness—some in coming, some in going.

Make one person happy each day and in forty years you will have made 14,000 human beings happy for a time at least. CHARLES WILEY

When someone does something good, applaud! You will make two people happy. SAMUEL GOLDWYN

Worry doesn't help tomorrow's troubles, but it does ruin today's happiness.

Happiness makes up in height for what it lacks in length. ROBERT FROST

To be busy is man's only happiness. MARK TWAIN

You are much happier when you are happy than when you ain't. OGDEN NASH

Make happy those who are near, and those who are far will come. CHINESE PROVERB

Happiness is a very small desk and a very big wastebasket. ROBERT ORBEN

Heart

As a face is reflected in water, so the
heart reflects the person.

PROVERBS 27:19

———

A glad heart makes a happy face; a
broken heart crushes the spirit.

PROVERBS 15:13

———

For the happy heart, life is a continual
feast.

PROVERBS 15:15

———

The crooked heart will not
prosper. . . . A cheerful heart is good
medicine, but a broken spirit saps a
person's strength.

PROVERBS 17:20, 22

———

It is senseless to pay tuition to
educate a fool who has no heart for
wisdom.

PROVERBS 17:16

Heart

It is not by the gray of the hair that one knows the age of the heart.
EDWARD BULWER-LYTTON

Believe it, you are a real find, a joy in someone's heart. You are a jewel, unique and priceless. God don't make no junk!
HERBERT BARKS

To handle yourself, use your head; to handle others, use your heart.

The smile that lights the face will also warm the heart.

Bernard Baruch once reminded us that two things are bad for the heart—running up stairs and running down people.

Don't forget that people will judge you by your actions, not your intentions. You may have a heart of gold—but so does a hard-boiled egg.

In judging others, it's always wise to see with the heart as well as with the eyes.

The way to a man's heart is through his stomach, but the way to a woman's heart is a buy-path.

Never worry about your heart till it stops beating.

When God measures a man, he puts the tape around his heart and not his head.

Sympathy is two hearts tugging at the same load.

Home

The curse of the Lord is on the house
of the wicked, but his blessing is on
the home of the upright.

PROVERBS 3:33

Home

Home is where the mortgage is!

Home—there's no place like it if you haven't got the money to go out.

Home—where part of the family waits until the rest brings back the car.

A modern home is one in which a switch regulates everything except the children.

Home is a place where a man is free to say anything he pleases because no one pays any attention to him anyhow.

'Mid pleasures and palaces
Though we may roam,
Be it ever so humble,
There's no place like home.

Strange development: before the wedding he wouldn't go home. After the wedding, he wouldn't stay home.

Father says they just bought a new all-electric home— everything in it is charged.

In these days when taxes are high, a man's home is his hassle.

A broken home is the world's greatest wreck.

Youngsters always brighten up a home. They forget to turn off the lights.

Home is where you hang your heart.

Houses are built of brick and stone, but homes are made of love alone.

A *Home Blueprint*

   Home—a world of strife shut out, a world of love shut in.
   Home—a place where the small are great, and the great
      are small.
   Home—the father's kingdom, the mother's world, and the
      child's paradise.
   Home—the place where we grumble the most, and are
      treated the best.
   Home—the center of our affection, round which our
      heart's best wishes twine.
   Home—the place where our stomachs get three square
      meals a day and our hearts a thousand. CHARLES M. CROW

Home is where you go when other places close. JOSEPH LAURIE

Home—the place where, when you go there, they have to take
you in.   ROBERT FROST

House—the thing that keeps a man running to the hardware
store.   ROBERT ZWICKERY

Honor

Fear of the Lord teaches a person to
be wise; humility precedes honor.

PROVERBS 15:33

———

It is an honor to receive
an honest reply.

PROVERBS 24:26

———

Honor your father and mother.

EXODUS 20:12

Honor

Honor lies in honest toil.   GROVER CLEVELAND

He has honor if he holds himself to an ideal of conduct though
it is inconvenient, unprofitable, or dangerous to do so.
                                                   WALTER LIPPMANN

The louder he talked of his honor, the faster we counted our
spoons.   RALPH WALDO EMERSON

Professor: "Now, this examination will be conducted on the
honor system. Please take seats three seats apart, in alternate
rows, and we shall begin."

I feel it is time I also pay tribute to my four writers—
Matthew, Mark, Luke and John.   BISHOP FULTON J. SHEEN

That nation is worthless that will not, with pleasure, venture
all for its honor.   JOHANN C. SCHILLER

It is better to deserve honors and not have them than to have
them and not deserve them.   MARK TWAIN

There's honor among thieves—at least until they begin to deal
with lawyers.

Less is sometimes more: honor is more than honors.

From our ancestors come our names; from our virtues, our
honors.   GROVER CLEVELAND

Live today and every day like a man of honor.   CHARLES ELIOT

Hope

In the same way, wisdom is sweet to your soul. If you find it, you will have a bright future, and your hopes will not be cut short.

PROVERBS 24:14

The hopes of the godly result in happiness, but the expectations of the wicked are all in vain.

PROVERBS 10:28

When the wicked die, their hopes all perish, for they rely on their own feeble strength.

PROVERBS 11:7

Hope deferred makes the heart sick, but when dreams come true, there is life and joy.

PROVERBS 13:12

Hope

Hope is the feeling that you will succeed tomorrow in what you failed at today.

Anyone can overcome depression. The first step is to simply realize that there is hope.

He who has health has hope, and he who has hope has everything.

Hope, like the gleaming taper's light,
   Adorns and cheers our way;
And still, as darker grows the night,
   Emits a lighter ray.
                          OLIVER GOLDSMITH

Hope springs eternal in the human breast:
Man never is, but always to be blest.
                          ALEXANDER POPE

Sam: "Have you ever realized any of your childhood hopes?"
Cam: "Yes, when mother used to comb my hair, I often wished I didn't have any."

The heart bowed down by weight of woe to weakest hope will cling.
                          ALFRED BUNN

Hope is that which makes us live today as if tomorrow were yesterday.

Life without hope is a life without meaning.

What oxygen is to the lungs, such is hope to the meaning of life.
                          EMIL BRUNNER

Hope smiles on the threshold of the year to come, whispering that it will be happier.
                    ALFRED, LORD TENNYSON

Humor

Laughter can conceal a heavy heart;
when the laughter ends,
the grief remains.

PROVERBS 14:13

———

There is a time for everything,
a season for every activity
under heaven. A time to cry and
a time to laugh.

ECCLESIASTES 3:1, 4

Humor

Humor is to life what shock absorbers are to automobiles.

The Bible speaks of a time when all tears shall be wiped away.
But it makes no mention of a time when we shall cease to
smile.   J. D. Eppinga

The humorist has a good eye for the humbug; he does not
always recognize the saint.   W. Somerset Maugham

A sense of humor is the lubricant of life's machinery.

Humor is the harmony of the heart.   Douglas Jerrold

Laughter is the tranquilizer with no side effects.
                                              Arnold Glasgow

Good humor is a tonic for mind and body. It is the best
antidote for anxiety and depression. It is a business asset. It
attracts and keeps friends. It lightens human burdens. It is the
direct route to serenity and contentment.   Grenville Kleider

Our five senses are incomplete without the sixth—a sense of
humor.

Laughter is part of the human survival kit.   David Nathan

The saving grace of America lies in the fact that the
overwhelming majority are possessed of two great qualities—
a sense of humor and a sense of proportion.
                                        Franklin D. Roosevelt

If you can look into the mirror without laughter, you have no
sense of humor.

Humility/Haughtiness

Haughtiness goes before destruction;
humility precedes honor.

PROVERBS 18:12

True humility and fear of the Lord
lead to riches, honor, and long life.

PROVERBS 22:4

Pride ends in humiliation, while
humility brings honor.

PROVERBS 29:23

Humility/Haughtiness

Few things are as humbling as a three-way mirror.

As the nightingale instinctively flees from the sound of the hawk, so does the beauty of humility vanish in the presence of pride. WILLIAM A. WARD

Humility is to make the right estimate of yourself. CHARLES SPURGEON

Don't be humble; you're not that great. GOLDA MEIR

The fellow who does things that count doesn't usually stop to count them.

One of the hardest secrets for a man to keep is his opinion of himself.

To be humble to superiors is duty; to equals, courtesy; to inferiors, nobility.

Those traveling the highway of humility won't be bothered by heavy traffic.

Sincere humility attracts. Lack of humility subtracts. Artificial humility detracts.

Humility is like underwear—essential, but indecent if it shows. HELEN NEILSON

I used to think that God's gifts were on shelves—one above the other and the taller we grew, the more easily we could reach them. I now find that God's gifts are on shelves one beneath the other and that it is not a question of growing taller but of stooping lower. F. B. MEYER

God created the world out of nothing, and as long as we are nothing, he can make something out of us.   MARTIN LUTHER

Humility is remaining teachable.

Humility is a strange thing; the moment you think you have it, you have lost it.

I long to accomplish a great and noble task, but it is my chief duty to accomplish humble tasks as though they were great and noble. The world is moved along, not only by the mighty shoves of its heroes, but also by the aggregate of the tiny pushes of each honest worker.   HELEN KELLER

There is a big difference between humility and stupidity.
ALFRED ARMAND MONTAPERT

The most thankful people are the humblest.

I believe the first test of a truly great man is his humility.
JOHN RUSKIN

Nothing sets a person so much out of the devil's reach as humility.   JONATHAN EDWARDS

The person with true humility never has to be shown his place; he is always in it.

Stay humble or stumble.

The best way to be right or wrong is humbly.

Humility is one of the qualities that is missing in the "self-made" man.

Humility is a wonderful trait, but it doesn't help you to get waited on in a crowded store.

The person who looks up to God rarely looks down on people.

Humility makes a man feel smaller as he becomes greater.

Humility is elusive. It is such a fragile plant that the slightest reference to it causes it to wilt and die.

Indolence

Lazy people want much but get little,
but those who work hard will prosper
and be satisfied.

PROVERBS 13:4

———

Take a lesson from the ants, you
lazybones. Learn from their ways and
be wise! Even though they have no
prince, governor, or ruler to make
them work, they labor hard all
summer, gathering food for the
winter. But you, lazybones, how long
will you sleep?

PROVERBS 6:6-9

Indolence

If you have time to lean, you have time to clean.

He's the kind of student with a Cadillac mind but a Pinto performance.

Poverty is usually the side-partner of laziness.

The quickest way to crush whatever laurels you have won is to rest on them.

The Sunday school teacher asked her class, "What parable do you like best?"
Little Johnny replied, "The one about the multitude that loafs and fishes."

A lazy boy and a warm bed are difficult to part.   DANISH PROVERB

To do nothing is in every man's power.   SAMUEL JOHNSON

Laziness grows on people; it begins in cobwebs and ends in iron chains.   M. HALE

"Son," said the boss to the lazy office boy, "I don't know how we're going to get along without you, but starting Monday we're going to try."

Indolence is a bodily affliction that mostly the young indulge in and only the old can afford.

Indolence is the mental alertness to avoid hard work.

The habit of resting before fatigue sets in is laziness.
JULES RENARD

Idleness is the refuge of weak minds, and the holiday of fools.

LORD CHESTERFIELD

He is idle who might be better employed.   THOMAS FULLER

The ruin of most men is idleness.   GEORGE HILLIARD

Idleness is stagnant satisfaction.   SAMUEL SMILES

Disciplined inaction is indolence.

Instruction/Learning

Those who listen to instruction will
prosper; those who trust the Lord will
be happy. The wise are known for
their understanding, and instruction
is appreciated if it's well presented.

PROVERBS 16:20-21

―――

The wise are glad to be instructed,
but babbling fools fall flat on
their faces.

PROVERBS 10:8

―――

Listen to the words of the wise; apply
your heart to my instruction. Commit
yourself to instruction.

PROVERBS 22:17; 23:12

―――

Teach the wise, and they will be wiser.
Teach the righteous, and they will
learn more.

PROVERBS 9:9

Instruction/Learning

A young applicant for a job as a truck driver for a Los Angeles dairy was asked if he was married. "No," he replied. "I'm not—but I can take orders, if that's what you mean."

The person who knows everything has a lot to learn.

Anyone who stops learning is old, whether this happens at twenty or eighty. Anyone who keeps on learning not only remains young, but becomes constantly more valuable regardless of physical capacity.   HARVEY ULLMAN

They know enough who know how to learn.   HENRY ADAMS

An Indian was persuaded to attend an instructional lecture. When it was all over, someone asked him what he thought of it. "Huh!" he grunted. "Big wind, lotta dust, no rain!"

As long as you live, keep learning how to live.   SENECA

Lose if you must, but don't lose the lesson.

Learn to say no and it will do you more good than being able to speak Latin.

No one is ever too old to learn, and that may be why all of us keep putting it off.

Integrity

Fire tests the purity of silver and gold,
but a person is tested by being
praised.

PROVERBS 27:21

———

The godly walk with integrity; blessed
are their children after them.

PROVERBS 20:7

———

Even children are known by the way
they act, whether their conduct is pure
and right.

PROVERBS 20:11

Integrity

Integrity is the basis of all true-blue success.   B. C. FORBES

The greatest danger facing the United States is not a military lag but a slump in personal and public integrity.

ROBERT J. MCCRACKEN

You cannot drive straight on a twisting lane.   RUSSIAN PROVERB

Always allow honesty and integrity to increase with your riches.

The integrity of men is to be measured by their conduct, not by their professions.   JUNIUS

Character is never erected on a neglected conscience.

Character is made by many acts; it may be lost by a single act.

Few things are more dangerous to a person's integrity than having nothing to do and plenty of time in which to do it.

Take care of your character, and your reputation will take care of itself.

Youth and beauty fade; integrity endures forever.

Reputation is what you need to get a job; character is what you need to keep it.

Good character, like good soup, is made at home.

Keeping Your Word

The Lord hates those who don't
keep their word, but he delights in
those who do.

PROVERBS 12:22

It is dangerous to make
a rash promise to God
before counting the cost.

PROVERBS 20:25

A person who doesn't give a promised
gift is like clouds and wind
that don't bring rain.

PROVERBS 25:14

So when you make a promise to God,
don't delay in following through, for
God takes no pleasure in fools.

ECCLESIASTES 5:4

Keeping Your Word

Vows are often made in storms and forgotten in calms.

Many promises impair confidence. LATIN PROVERB

A promise made is a debt unpaid. WILLIAM SHAKESPEARE

Promises may get friends, but it is performance that keeps them. OWEN FELTHAM

In the land of promise a man may die of hunger. DUTCH PROVERB

Magnificent promises are always to be suspected. THEODORE PARKER

He who is slow in promising is always the most faithful in performing. ROUSSEAU

Promises are like money—easier made than kept.

If you promise less and do more, your boss will eventually put your name on a door.

Do not vow—our love is frail as is our life, and full as little in our power. SIR GEORGE ETHEREGE

When you break your word, you break something that cannot be mended.

Promises are like crying babies in church—they should be carried out immediately.

One thing you can give and still keep is your word.

Kindness

Your own soul is nourished when you are kind, but you destroy yourself when you are cruel.

PROVERBS 11:17

———

Never let loyalty and kindness get away from you! Wear them like a necklace; write them deep within your heart.

PROVERBS 3:3

Kindness

Hatred and anger are powerless when met with kindness.

Let me be a little kinder, let me be a little blinder to the faults of those around me.   EDGAR A. GUEST

Kindness is the oil that takes the friction out of life.

A kind heart is a fountain of gladness, making everything in its vicinity freshen into smiles.   WASHINGTON IRVING

'Twas a thief said the last word to Christ: Christ took the kindness and forgave the theft.   ROBERT BROWNING

Kindness has converted more sinners than zeal, eloquence or learning.   FREDERICK W. FABER

Kindness put off until tomorrow may become only a bitter regret.

Be kind to unkind people—they need it the most.

A kind word is better than a handout.

Life is short, and we have never too much time for gladdening the hearts of those who are traveling the dark journey with us. Oh, be swift to love, make haste to be kind!
                                           HENRI FRÉDÉRIC AMIEL

Kindness pays most when you don't do it for pay.

Knowledge/Education

Then you will understand what it means to fear the Lord, and you will gain knowledge of God. For the Lord grants wisdom! From his mouth come knowledge and understanding.

PROVERBS 2:5-6

A mocker seeks wisdom and never finds it, but knowledge comes easily to those with understanding.

PROVERBS 14:6

The Lord preserves knowledge, but he ruins the plans of the deceitful.

PROVERBS 22:12

A wise man is mightier than a strong man, and a man of knowledge is more powerful than a strong man.

PROVERBS 24:5

Knowledge/Education

A bird can sing on a perch that swings because he knows how to fly.

He who has a strange horse goes halfway on foot.

Some students drink at the fountain of knowledge—others just gargle.

I know where charity begins,
But since the first lend-leases
I've wondered more and more,
Just where this painful virtue ceases.   Francis O. Walsh

Describing his friend, the man said, "He knows so little and knows it so fluently!"

If you want to get into *Who's Who,* you'd better first learn what's what.

As for me, all I know is that I know nothing.   Socrates

Like the surgeon said—"It's fifty dollars for cuttin' and a full hundred for knowin' where."

Education is forcing abstract ideas into concrete heads.

Schoolhouses are the republican line of fortifications.
                                                        Horace Mann

It's not only the IQ but also the I Will that is important in getting an education.

I've never let my schooling interfere with my education.

MARK TWAIN

Training is everything. The peach was once a bitter almond; cauliflower is but a cabbage with a college education.

MARK TWAIN

Education covers a lot of ground, but it doesn't cultivate it.

Labor

The desires of lazy people will be
their ruin, for their hands refuse
to work.

PROVERBS 21:25

———

Hard workers have plenty of food;
playing around brings poverty.

PROVERBS 28:19

———

If you are too lazy to plow in the right
season, you will have no food at the
harvest.

PROVERBS 20:4

———

It is good for workers to have an
appetite; an empty stomach drives
them on.

PROVERBS 16:26

Labor

If you want a place in the sun, be willing to expect some blisters.　　　　　　　　　　　　　　　　　ROB HATTEN

Some people remind us of blisters; they show up after the work is done.

Success is sweet, but its secret is sweat.

The more you sweat in peace, the less you bleed in war.
　　　　　CHINESE PROVERB USED BY GEN. NORMAN SCHWARZKOPF
　　　　　　　　　　AT THE NAVAL ACADEMY GRADUATION, 1991

If you work for a man, for heaven's sake, work for him.
　　　　　　　　　　　　　　　　　　　　KIN HUBBARD

A pint of sweat will save a gallon of blood.　　GEORGE PATTON JR.

I know hard work never hurt anyone, but I'm not taking any chances.

The supermarket bag boy was asked, "How long have you been working here?"
He replied, "Ever since they threatened to fire me!"

We have two classes in this country: the working class, and the one whose teacher has left the room for a few minutes.
　　　　　　　　　　　　　　　　　　　　FRANK WALSH

Why is it that some people stop working as soon as they find a job?

Let us be grateful to Adam, our benefactor. He cut us out of the "blessing" of idleness and won for us the "curse" of labor.
　　　　　　　　　　　　　　　　　　　　MARK TWAIN

Far and away the best prize that life offers is the chance to work hard at work worth doing. THEODORE ROOSEVELT

In time you may perhaps find that most of the work of the world is done by people who aren't feeling very well.
LE BARON RUSSELL BRIGGS

Here's a stubborn truth
On which you can bet:
The harder you work,
The luckier you get. L. J. HUBER

The worst day of fishing beats the best day of work.

He who wishes to eat in the evening must be willing to work earlier in the day.

Leisure and I have parted company. I am resolved to be busy till I die. JOHN WESLEY

The trouble with a husband who works like a horse is that all he wants to do in the evenings is hit the hay.

He who fiddles around seldom gets to lead the orchestra.

Confession: When I have the urge to work, I lie down until it goes away.

Now I get me up to work;
    I pray the Lord I may not shirk,
And if I die before tonight,
    I pray my work will be all right. DONALD SHARP

The desire to work is so rare that it must be encouraged wherever it is found. ABRAHAM LINCOLN

The reason worry kills more people than work is that more people worry than work.   ROBERT FROST

There aren't any hard-and-fast rules for getting ahead in this world—just hard ones.

Salesman: "This machine will cut your work in half."
Customer: "Great! I'll take two!"

A city boy spent his first night on a farm. Much earlier than usual, he was awakened by the activity around him. He remarked sleepily, "It doesn't take long to stay here all night, does it?"

Work never tires me. Idleness exhausts me completely.
    SHERLOCK HOLMES

Most of us aren't really workaholics. Think about it: Have you ever heard of a Thank-God-It's-Monday Club?

It's difficult to soar with eagles when you have to work with turkeys.

Law/Justice

When people do not accept divine guidance, they run wild. But whoever obeys the law is happy.

PROVERBS 29:18

———

To reject the law is to praise the wicked; to obey the law is to fight them. Young people who obey the law are wise; those who seek out worthless companions bring shame to their parents. The prayers of a person who ignores the law are despised.

PROVERBS 28:4, 7, 9

Law/Justice

Laws too gentle are seldom obeyed; too severe, seldom executed.   BENJAMIN FRANKLIN

The welfare of the people is the highest law.   CICERO

I sometimes wish that people would put a little more emphasis on the observance of the law than they do on its enforcement.   CALVIN COOLIDGE

No law has ever been passed that will keep a man from acting the fool.

Men fight for freedom and then start making laws to get rid of it.

Never forget the fact that ignorance of the law is what keeps our higher courts functioning.

Of all the laws we have to contend with, the most troublesome are usually the in-laws.

The arm of the law needs a little more muscle.

Too many laws are passed—then bypassed.

Where law ends, tyranny begins.   WILLIAM PITT

We need tougher child abuse laws; parents have taken enough abuse from their children.

Strict enforcement of the law against pollution of the air should result in fewer, shorter, and better political speeches.

Leadership

Without wise leadership, a nation
falls; with many counselors,
there is safety.

PROVERBS 11:14

———

Work hard and become a leader;
be lazy and become a slave.

PROVERBS 12:24

Leadership

There are no office hours for leaders.   JAMES CARDINAL GIBBONS

Nearly all born leaders of men are women.

The trouble with being a leader today is that you can't be sure whether people are following you or chasing you.

A leader has two important characteristics: first, he knows where he is going; second, he is able to persuade other people to go with him.

A real leader faces the music when he doesn't like the tune.
ARNOLD H. GLASSGOW

He who follows the leader won't be following the follower.

He who stands at the head of the line must know where he's going.

Keep your fears to yourself, but share your courage with others.   ROBERT LOUIS STEVENSON

Being a general calls for different talents from being a soldier.
TITUS LIVY

Leaders think. They think because they are leaders. They are leaders because they think.   PAUL PARKER

Leaders go down in history—some farther than others.

For a community leader, life is one big bowl of charities.

The world would be happier if its leaders had more vision and fewer nightmares.

It's extremely difficult to lead farther than you have gone yourself.

We herd sheep; we drive cattle; we lead men.

Lies/Truth

Truth stands the test of time; lies are soon exposed. An honest witness tells the truth; a false witness tells lies.

PROVERBS 12:19, 17

———

A truthful witness saves lives, but a false witness is a traitor.

PROVERBS 14:25

———

A wise person is hungry for truth, while the fool feeds on trash.

PROVERBS 15:14

———

Telling lies about others is as harmful as hitting them with an ax, wounding them with a sword, or shooting them with a sharp arrow.

PROVERBS 25:18

Lies/Truth

No man has a good enough memory to make a successful liar.
ABRAHAM LINCOLN

Some people tell the truth, and others say he's in conference just now.

Mirror, mirror, on the wall,
You're not pleasing me at all;
I know you cannot lie, forsooth,
But can't you slightly bend the truth?   NORA B. KATHRINS

You don't need such a good memory if you always speak the truth.

Truth is stubborn. It doesn't apologize to anyone.

He who is a liar needs a good memory.

Truth is not always popular, but it is always right.

I don't want any yes-men around me. I want everyone to tell me the truth—even though it costs him his job.
SAMUEL GOLDWYN

Truth has only to exchange hands a few times to become fiction.

Stretching the truth won't make it last any longer.

If you ever have something bad to say about anybody, be sure the answer to these three questions is yes before you say it. Is it true? Is it just? Will it do anybody any good to say it?

Show me a liar, and I'll show you a thief.   FRENCH PROVERB

The biggest liar in the world is "they say."

If you tell the truth, you don't have to remember anything.
MARK TWAIN

Liquor

Wine produces mockers; liquor leads
to brawls. Whoever is led astray by
drink cannot be wise.

PROVERBS 20:1

———

The person who strays from common
sense will end up in the company of
the dead.

PROVERBS 21:16

Liquor

Take one reckless natural-born fool, two or three drinks of liquor, and a fast, high-powered car. Soak fool in liquor, place in car, and let go. After due time, remove from wreckage, place in satin-lined box, and garnish with flowers.

Liquor won't wash away troubles; it will only irrigate them a little.

A sour-faced wife is a liquor dealer's friend.

I've noticed at cocktail parties,
    When it's taken to excess,
Liquor removes the polish
    From both furniture and guests.

Never yet have we seen a fellow who could keep himself and his business liquid at the same time.

A pink elephant is a beast of bourbon.

At the punchbowl's brink
    Let the thirsty think
What they say in Japan:
    "First the man takes a drink,
    Then the drink takes the drink,
    Then the drink takes the man!"   EDWARD ROWLAND SILL

Hangover: the moaning after the night before.

A drinking man commits suicide on the installment plan.

Cocktail party: A gathering where people drink martinis, spear olives, stab friends, and spill the beans.

We drink to one another's health,
    And yet before we've finished
Our round of toasts, our state of health
    Has noticeably diminished.

Only weak characters lean on strong drink!

Boozers are losers!

There are two finishes for automobiles: lacquer and liquor.

When we hear a man boasting about how much liquor he can hold, we get a mental picture of an animated garbage can.

Glasses can make driving a lot safer. Providing, of course, that they're worn instead of emptied.

A college is truly a fountain of knowledge, and a great many go there to drink.

People who say that many things drive them to drink should walk.

Accidents happen every hunting season because both hunter and gun are loaded.

To escape alcoholism is simple. Never take the drink just before the second one.

Yes, liquor still is digging graves.
    Of multitudes it first enslaves;
It's breaking hearts and bringing sighs
    And wringing tears from many eyes!

Why battle your way to the top and bottle your way to the bottom?

There's nothing wrong with drinking like a fish, provided you drink what a fish drinks.

It never fails: men who go out drinking leave as fit as a fiddle but come home tight as a drum.

A drunk is someone who goes into a bar optimistically and leaves misty optically.

Alcoholics are people who don't no when they've had enough.

An alcoholic musician is someone who can't get past the first bar.

Liquor is a substance that makes married men see double and feel single.

One reason I don't drink is that I want to know when I'm having a good time.

No alcoholic is really anonymous.

Four reasons for not drinking: the head is clearer, the health is better, the heart is lighter, and the purse is heavier.

When a man drinks too much liquor, he can approach you from several directions at once.

A weak moment with the bottle can mean several weeks in the jug.

One gallon of gas plus one pint of liquor often add up to a first-class funeral.

Listening

Fools think they need no advice, but
the wise listen to others.

PROVERBS 12:15

———

Wisdom shouts in the streets. . . .
"You simpletons!" she cries. "How
long will you go on being
simpleminded? . . . How long will you
fools fight the facts? Come here and
listen to me! I'll pour out the spirit
of wisdom upon you and make
you wise."

PROVERBS 1:20-23

Listening

The only reason some people listen to reason is to gain time for a rebuttal.

A good listener is not only popular everywhere, but after a while he knows something.   WILSON MIZNER

Formula for handling people:

    1. Listen to the other person's story.
    2. Listen to the other person's full story.
    3. Listen to the other person's story first. GEORGE MARSHALL

From listening comes wisdom, and from speaking, repentance.   ITALIAN PROVERB

Nothing makes a person such a good listener as eavesdropping.   FRANKLIN P. JONES

One of the best ways to persuade others is by listening to them.   DEAN RUSK

Musicians who play by ear should remember that we listen the same way.

If a man wants his wife to listen, he should talk to another woman.

Looking for the solution without listening to the problem is working in the dark.

It takes courage to stand up and speak, as well as to sit down and listen.

Give every man thy ear, but few thy voice. WILLIAM SHAKESPEARE

Listen—or thy tongue will keep thee deaf.
AMERICAN-INDIAN PROVERB

It is important for a good manager to know how to listen as well as to talk. We too often forget that communication is an exchange. LEE IACOCCA

Half an hour's listening is essential except when you are very busy. Then a full hour is needed. ST. FRANCIS DE SALES

Husband, calling his wife to the phone: "Dear, somebody wants to listen to you!"

Too many of us have not learned to listen. Poor listeners range all the way from the impatient type—"That's nothing! Wait'll you hear what I've done!"—to the person so absorbed in his own thoughts that he is not aware that someone has spoken. Learning to listen actively, and constructively, is as important as learning to speak, if communication is to be effective. WILLIAM C. TACEY

It's hard to listen while you're planning something you think needs to be said.

I have no voice for singing, I cannot make a speech;
I have no gift for music, I know I cannot teach.
I am no good at leading, I cannot "organize,"
And anything that I would write would never win a prize.
It seems my only talent is neither big nor rare—
Just to listen and encourage, and to fill a vacant chair.

In this country you are still privileged to free speech but that's as far as the Constitution goes. It doesn't guarantee listeners.

God still speaks to those who take time to listen.

Take a tip from nature—your ears aren't made to shut, but your mouth is!

Love

Whoever pursues godliness and
unfailing love will find life,
godliness, and honor.

PROVERBS 21:21

———

Hatred stirs up quarrels, but love
covers all offenses.

PROVERBS 10:12

———

Disregarding another person's faults
preserves love; telling about them
separates close friends.

PROVERBS 17:9

Love

To love someone is to seek his or her best and highest good.

I have learned that only two things are necessary to keep one's wife happy. First, let her think she is having her way. And, second, let her have it.   LYNDON B. JOHNSON

Love is friendship set to music.   CHANNING POLLOCK

Love is the basic need of human nature, for without it, life is disrupted emotionally, mentally, spiritually and physically.
      KARL MENNINGER

When love and skill work together, expect a masterpiece.
      CHARLES READE

Love without return is like a question without an answer.

'Tis better to have loved and lost
Than never to have loved at all.   ALFRED, LORD TENNYSON

Don't underestimate love at first sight. Many of us might not pass a second inspection.

Love is a fabric that never fades, no matter how often it is washed in the waters of adversity and grief.

He drew a circle that shut me out—
Heretic, rebel, a thing to flout.
But love and I had the wit to win;
We drew a circle that took him in.   EDWIN MARKHAM

The girl who thinks no man is good enough for her may be right, but more often she is left.

One of our greatest learning tasks is how to give and receive love.

The love we give away is the only love we keep.   ELBERT HUBBARD

A sultan at odds with his harem
Thought of a way he could scarem,
He caught a gray mouse,
Turned it loose in the house,
And started the first harem scarem.

Love is said to be blind, but I know lots of fellows in love who
can see twice as much in their sweethearts as I can.

JOSH BILLINGS

He gave her a look that you could have poured on a waffle.

RING LARDNER

Love is a form of insanity that makes a girl marry her boss and
work for him the rest of her life without salary.

Naturally no one ever gives the groom a shower—he's all
washed up anyway.   J. W. PELKIE

The first thing a girl hopes for from the garden of love is at
least one carat.   S. S. BIDDLE

Love is not only something you feel. It's something you do.

DAVID WILKERSON

Ironic, isn't it, that in tennis "love" is nothing but in life
"love" is everything!

A bell is not a bell until you ring it;
A song is not a song until you sing it.
Love in your heart is not put there to stay;
Love is not love until you give it away.   OSCAR HAMMERSTEIN II

Love is seeking to make another person happy.

173

Loyalty

Don't ask me to leave you and turn
back. I will go wherever you go and
live wherever you live. Your people
will be my people, and your God will
be my God. . . . May the Lord punish
me severely if I allow anything but
death to separate us!

RUTH, RUTH 1:16-17

———

Loyalty makes a person attractive.
And it is better to be poor than
dishonest.

PROVERBS 19:22

———

Many will say they are loyal friends,
but who can find one who is
really faithful?

PROVERBS 20:6

Loyalty

We are all the President's men.   HENRY KISSINGER

If you are not too long, I will wait for you all my life.
                                                       OSCAR WILDE

There is one element that is worth its weight in gold and that
is loyalty. It will cover a multitude of weaknesses.
                                                       PHILIP ARMOUR

Lack of loyalty is one of the major causes of failure in every
walk of life.   NAPOLEON HILL

Loyalty is rare. It can only be proven under test.
                                          ALFRED ARMAND MONTAPERT

Histories are more full of examples of the fidelity of dogs than
of friends.   ALEXANDER POPE

If virtues be grades, loyalty, I think, would stand near the top
of the list. At any rate, no leader can demonstrate his full
capabilities without it.   A. P. GOUTHEY

Often loyalty consists of keeping your mouth shut.

It is better to be faithful than famous.   THEODORE ROOSEVELT

We are all in the same boat in a stormy sea, and we owe each
other a terrible loyalty.   G. K. CHESTERTON

Loyalty in little things is a great thing.

Marriage

Drink water from your own
well—share your love only with your
wife. Let your wife be a fountain of
blessing for you.

PROVERBS 5:15, 18

———

A worthy wife is her husband's joy and
crown; a shameful wife saps
his strength.

PROVERBS 12:4

———

The man who finds a wife finds a
treasure and receives favor from the
Lord. A nagging wife annoys like a
constant dripping. It is better to live
alone in the corner of an attic than
with a contentious wife in a lovely
home. It is better to live alone in the
desert than with a crabby,
complaining wife.

PROVERBS 18:22; 19:13; 21:9, 19

Marriage

A happy marriage is a long conversation which always seems too short.   ANDRE MAUROIS

The husband who wants a happy marriage should learn to keep his mouth shut and his checkbook open.   GROUCHO MARX

A man without a wife is but half a man.

Praise marriage not on the third day but after the third year.

He who marries for wealth sells his own liberty.

As most veterans will tell you, marriage is the continuous process of getting used to things you hadn't expected.

Marriage resembles a pair of shears, so joined that they cannot be separated; often moving in opposite directions, yet always punishing anyone who comes between them.

SYDNEY SMITH

There is one phase of life that I have
   Never heard discussed in any seminar,
And that is all women think men
   Are funny and all men think that weminar.   OGDEN NASH

Marriage would work out better if both sides would operate not only on the fifty-fifty basis but on the thrifty-thrifty basis as well.

Marriage has some thorns, but celibacy has no roses.

My most brilliant achievement was my ability to be able to persuade my wife to marry me.   WINSTON CHURCHILL

Wife: be to his virtues kind; be to his faults a little blind.

The most difficult years of marriage are those following the wedding.

Love often intoxicates; marriage always sobers.

Marriage is like the army—many complain, but you'd be surprised how many reenlist.

Love is never having to say you're sorry. Marriage is never having a chance to say anything.

Keep the eyes wide open before marriage and half shut afterwards.   BENJAMIN FRANKLIN

Often the difference between a successful marriage and a mediocre one consists of leaving about three or four things a day unsaid.   HARLAN MILLER

To keep your marriage brimming,
    With love in the loving cup,
Whenever you're wrong, admit it,
    Whenever you're right, shut up.   OGDEN NASH

An ideal marriage is one in which two people love, cherish, and encourage each other through all the troubles caused by their marriage.

They were married for better or worse. He couldn't have done better, and she could have done worse.

There would be a lot more happy marriages if husbands tried to understand their wives and wives tried to understand football.

Love is blind, and marriage is an eye-opener.

A fool and his money are soon married.

Motivation

The Lord's searchlight penetrates the human spirit, exposing every hidden motive. God loathes the sacrifice of an evil person, especially when it is brought with ulterior motives.

PROVERBS 20:27; 21:27

People may think they are doing what is right, but the Lord examines the heart.

PROVERBS 21:2

Motivation

Motives are invisible but they are the true test of character.
ALFRED ARMAND MONTAPERT

Other people see your deeds. God sees your motives.

One motivation is worth ten threats, two pressures and six reminders.
PAUL SWEENEY

The noblest motive is the public good.
VIRGIL

The biggest gap in the world is the gap between the justice of a cause and the motives of the people pushing it.
JOHN P. GRIER

It is motive alone that gives character to the actions of men.
JEAN DE LA BRUYÉRE

We would often be ashamed of our best actions if the world only knew the motives behind them.
FRANÇOIS DE LA ROCHEFOUCAULD

One must not lose desires. They are mighty stimulants to creativeness, to love, and to long life.
A. A. BOGOMOLETZ

Every man without passions has within him no principle of action, nor motive to act.
CLAUDE-ADRIEN HELVÉTIUS

It is a horrible demoralizing thing to be a lawyer. You look for such low motives in everyone and everything.
KATHERINE T. HINKSON

Reason is the wise man's guide; example, the fool's.
WELSH PROVERB

Neighbors

Do not withhold good from those who deserve it when it's in your power to help them. If you can help your neighbor now, don't say, "Come back tomorrow, and then I'll help you."

PROVERBS 3:27-28

———

Do not plot against your neighbors, for they trust you. Don't make accusations against someone who hasn't wronged you.

PROVERBS 3:29-30

———

Evil people love to harm others; their neighbors get no mercy from them.

PROVERBS 21:10

———

Do not testify spitefully against innocent neighbors; don't lie about them.

PROVERBS 24:28

Neighbors

A neighbor is a person who can get to your house in less than a minute and takes two hours to go back home.   O. A. BATTISTA

Every man's neighbor is his looking glass.   ENGLISH PROVERB

When your neighbor's house is on fire, your own property is at stake.

It's easier to love humanity as a whole than to love your neighbor in particular.

We make our friends, we make our enemies, but God makes our next-door neighbor.   G. K. CHESTERTON

Americans sink millions of dollars in unsound financial schemes, one of which is trying to keep up with the neighbors.

Nothing depreciates a car faster than having a neighbor buy a new one.

The ideal neighbor is the one who makes noise at the same time as we do.

You don't have to be an accomplished musician to play on your neighbors' nerves.

A good neighbor doubles the value of a house.   GERMAN PROVERB

I do not ask for mighty words
   To leave the crowd impressed;
But grant my life may ring so true,
   My neighbor may be blessed.

Opinion/Stand

Fools have no interest in
understanding; they only want to air
their own opinions.

PROVERBS 18:2

———

The Lord demands fairness in every
business deal; he sets the standard.

PROVERBS 16:11

———

The Lord despises double standards of
every kind. He is not pleased by
dishonest scales.

PROVERBS 20:10, 23

Opinion/Stand

Some people fall for everything and stand for nothing.

The foolish and the dead never change their opinions.
                                        JAMES RUSSELL LOWELL

Stand on your own two feet and you will grow in stature.

The trouble with letting people know where you stand is that
you become a stationary target.   MARLYS HUFFMAN

Most of us like a person who comes right out and says what he
thinks—especially when he thinks what we think.

Opinionated people: little rotund islands of complacency
anchored in a sea of prejudices.

The fellow who has a good opinion of himself is likely a poor
judge of human nature.

A ninety-pound weakling took a medical examination. At the
end, he asked, "Well, doctor, how do I stand?"
"I don't know," replied the doctor. "It's a miracle!"

Our strength is shown in the things we stand for; our weakness
is shown in the things we fall for.

Stand firm for what you know is right
It's wise, as I have found.
The mighty oak was once a nut
That simply held its ground.   AGNES W. THOMAS

It is human to stand with the crowd; it is divine to stand
alone.

If your dog thinks you're the greatest person in the world, don't seek a second opinion.

Doctor to concerned patient: "I don't know why you wanted a second opinion. Your doctor's guess is as good as mine."

Everyone is entitled to my opinion.

Don't just stand there—*undo* something.

Opportunity

A wise youth works hard all summer; a youth who sleeps away the hour of opportunity brings shame.

PROVERBS 10:5

Opportunity

An opportunist is someone who teaches the children to swim when the basement is flooded.

The trouble with opportunity is that it's always more recognizable going than coming.

The sure way to miss success is to miss the opportunity.

VICTOR CHARLES

In the fields of opportunity it's always plowing time.

Opportunity knocks, but it has never been known to turn the knob and walk in.

Make hay while the sun shines.

ENGLISH PROVERB

He who kills time buries opportunities.

When one door closes, another opens; but we often look so long and so regretfully upon the closed door that we do not see the one which has opened for us.   ALEXANDER GRAHAM BELL

Be grateful for the doors of opportunity, and for the friends who oil the hinges.

Luck is what happens when preparation meets opportunity.

No business opportunity is ever lost. If you fumble it, your competitor will find it.

When opportunity knocks, the grumbler complains about the noise.

Parents

Parents can provide their sons with an
inheritance of houses and wealth, but
only the Lord can give an
understanding wife.

PROVERBS 19:14

What a pleasure it is to have wise
children. So give your parents joy!

PROVERBS 23:24-25

It is painful to be the parent of a fool;
there is no joy for the father of a
rebel. A foolish child brings grief to a
father and bitterness to a mother.

PROVERBS 17:21, 25

Discipline your children, and they
will give you happiness and peace
of mind.

PROVERBS 29:17

Parents

In a school essay on parents, one little girl wrote: "We get our parents when they are so old it is hard to change their habits."

Parenthood is the art of bringing up children without putting them down.

Children are a great comfort in one's old age, which one would not reach so quickly if one didn't have children.

The best time for parents to put the children to bed is while they still have the strength. HOMER PHILLIPS

Parents can give everything but common sense.

YIDDISH PROVERB

He who takes the child by the hand takes the mother by the heart. GERMAN PROVERB

The experts and we
Can never agree.
They say children are ruined
Before they are three.

But we'll keep on trying
We'll valiantly strive
To rehabilitate Junior
Before he is five. LOUISE DARCY

If discipline was practiced in every home, juvenile delinquency would be reduced by 95 percent. J. EDGAR HOOVER

Good parents are not afraid to be momentarily disliked by children during the act of enforcing rules. JEAN LAIRD

Spare the rod and spoil the child—that is true. But, beside the rod, keep an apple to give him when he has done well.

MARTIN LUTHER

When parents don't mind that the children don't mind, then children don't.

The actions of some children today suggest that their parents embarked upon the seas of matrimony without a paddle.

A child's back must be made to bend, but not be broken. He must be ruled, but not with a rod of iron. His spirit must be conquered, but not crushed.

CHARLES SPURGEON

Children are the sum of what parents contribute to their lives.

RICHARD L. STRAUSS

Parents spend half their time wondering how their children will turn out and half their time wondering when they will turn in.

Children aren't happy with nothing to ignore, and that's what parents are created for.

OGDEN NASH

Patience

Be glad for all God is planning
for you. Be patient in trouble,
and always be prayerful.

ROMANS 12:12

———

Dear brothers and sisters, you must be
patient as you wait for the Lord's
return. Consider the farmers who
eagerly look for the rains in the fall
and in the spring. They patiently wait
for the precious harvest to ripen. You,
too, must be patient. And take
courage, for the coming of
the Lord is near.

JAMES 5:7-8

Patience

Patience is the ability to count down before blasting off.

The horn of plenty is the one the guy behind you has on his car.

If you are patient in one amount of anger, you will escape a hundred days of sorrow. CHINESE PROVERB

Sign in a Texas country store: "Be patient. None of us am perfect!"

I wanted to be a doctor, but I didn't have any patience.

Impatient people always get there too late. JEAN DUTOURD

You must have patience on a diet—especially if it's your wife who's on it.

They also serve who only stand and wait. JOHN MILTON

We must learn that, like farmers, we can't sow and reap the same day.

Patience is a virtue that carries a lot of wait.

Bean by bean the bag is filled.

Adopt the pace of nature: Her secret is patience.
RALPH WALDO EMERSON

Be patient when a person growls at you; he may be living with a bear!

Patriotism

Without wise leadership, a nation falls; with many counselors, there is safety. Godliness exalts a nation, but sin is a disgrace to any people. When there is moral rot within a nation, its government topples easily. But with wise and knowledgeable leaders, there is stability.

PROVERBS 11:14; 14:34; 28:2

———

When the godly are in authority, the people rejoice. But when the wicked are in power, they groan. A just king gives stability to his nation, but one who demands bribes destroys it. When the wicked are in authority, sin increases. But the godly will live to see the tyrant's downfall.

PROVERBS 29:2, 4, 16

Patriotism

There's no trick to being a humorist when you have the whole
government working for you.   WILL ROGERS

I'll tell you folks, all politics is applesauce.   WILL ROGERS

An elephant is a mouse built to government specifications.

Dealing with bureaucracy is like trying to nail jelly to the wall.
JOHN F. KENNEDY

Congress passes bills, and the taxpayers pay them.

People ask me where I get my jokes. I just watch Congress and
report the facts; I don't even have to exaggerate.   WILL ROGERS

Government is like a big baby. An alimentary canal with a big
appetite at one end and no sense of responsibility at the other.
RONALD REAGAN

Just be glad you're not getting all the government you're
paying for.   WILL ROGERS

April 15 is the day millions of Americans feel bled, white and
blue.   ANN HERBERT

There are some politicians who, if their constituents were
cannibals, would promise them missionaries for dinner.
H. L. MENCKEN

Government is too big and too important to be left to the
politicians.   CHESTER BOWLES

The government is the only known vessel that leaks from the top. JAMES RESTON

Congress is so strange. A man gets up to speak and says nothing. Nobody listens—and then everybody disagrees.
  BORIS MARCHALOV

A silent majority and government by the people are incompatible. TOM HAYDEN

A statesman is any politician who isn't considered safe to name a school after. BILL VAUGHAN

Politics is like football. If you see daylight, go through the hole. JOHN F. KENNEDY

The difference between a politician and a statesman is: A politician thinks of the next election, and a statesman thinks of the next generation. JAMES F. CLARKE

When you think of having a woman as president, that's no problem. What's worrisome is the thought of having a man as the first lady.

The statesman shears the sheep; the politician skins them.
  AUSTIN O'MALLEY

A congressman ought to be limited to one term; then make him come home and live under the laws he helped pass.

Let Wall Street have a nightmare and the whole country has to help them back to bed again. WILL ROGERS

Blessed are the young, for they shall inherit the national debt.
  HERBERT HOOVER

Politics is perhaps the only profession for which no preparation is thought necessary. ROBERT L. STEVENSON

When I was a boy I was told that anybody could become president; I'm beginning to believe it. CLARENCE DARROW

What this country needs is more unemployed politicians.
EDWARD LANGLEY

America: Where there are ten million laws to enforce the Ten Commandments.

It is impossible to rightly govern the world without God and the Bible. GEORGE WASHINGTON

The Bible is worth all other books which have ever been printed. PATRICK HENRY

That Book, sir, is the rock on which our republic rests.
ANDREW JACKSON

Peace

But all who listen to me will live in peace and safety, unafraid of harm.

PROVERBS 1:33

A dry crust eaten in peace is better than a great feast with strife.

PROVERBS 17:1

God blesses those who work for peace, for they will be called the children of God.

JESUS, MATTHEW 5:9

Peace

Sign in Southern psychiatrist's office: Y'all calm!

The amazing thing about a man being arrested for disturbing the peace these days is that he could find any.

Keeping peace in the family requires patience, love, understanding—and at least two television sets.

The best way for a housewife to have a few peaceful moments to herself at the close of the day is to start doing the dishes.

All men desire peace, but very few desire those things that make for peace.   THOMAS À KEMPIS

Peace is the luxury you enjoy between your children's bedtime and your own.   LESTER D. KLIMEK

When at night you cannot sleep, talk to the Shepherd and stop counting sheep.

What the world needs is peace that passes all misunderstanding.

No God, no peace; know God, know peace.

There will be no peace as long as God remains unseated at the conference table.

Peace, like charity, begins at home.   FRANKLIN D. ROOSEVELT

Perseverance

They may trip seven times, but each time they will rise again. But one calamity is enough to lay the wicked low.

PROVERBS 24:16

———

Lazy people don't even cook the game they catch, but the diligent make use of everything they find.

PROVERBS 12:27

Perseverance

Perseverance has been defined as sticking to something you're not stuck on.

Perseverance is the result of a strong will. Obstinacy is the result of a strong "won't."

Our greatest glory is not in never falling but in rising every time we fall.

The road to success runs uphill, so don't expect to break any speed records.

The secret of success is to start from scratch and keep on scratching.

Our greatest weakness lies in giving up. The most certain way to succeed is always to try one more time.   THOMAS EDISON

It is my belief that talent is plentiful, and that what is lacking is staying power.   DORIS LESSING

A diamond is a chunk of coal that stuck to its job.

Better the shoulder to the wheel than the back to the wall.

It's often the last key on the ring that opens the door.

I hold a doctrine to which I owe much, indeed, but all the little I ever had, namely, that with ordinary talent and extraordinary perseverance all things are attainable.   T. F. BUXTON

He who starts many things finishes nothing.

We conquer—not in any brilliant fashion—we conquer by continuing.
GEORGE MATHESON

He who stops at third base to congratulate himself will never score a home run.

The game isn't over till it's over.
LAWRENCE PETER "YOGI" BERRA

Pessimism/Optimism

The fears of the wicked will all come
true; so will the hopes of the godly.

PROVERBS 10:24

Pessimism/Optimism

A pessimist looks at life through morose-colored glasses.

A miserable pessimist is one who took advice from an optimist.

Pessimists think the sun sets in the morning.

A pessimist is an optimist who endeavored to practice what he preached.

Because you have occasional low spells of despondency, don't despair. The sun has a sinking spell every night but it rises again all right the next morning.   HENRY VAN DYKE

A pessimist is a person who is always good for bad news, is never happy unless he's miserable, and burns his bridges before he gets to them.

A pessimist says the lily belongs to the onion family; an optimist declares that the onion belongs to the lily family.

Pessimist: one who, when he has a choice of two evils, chooses both.   OSCAR WILDE

A pessimist is an optimist who thought he could buy something for a dollar.

The man who is a pessimist before forty-eight knows too much; the man who is an optimist after forty-eight knows too little.

In the long run, the pessimist may be proved right; but the optimist has a better time on the trip.   DANIEL L. REARDON

The worst pest in the world is a pessimist; he sees only the mist.

'Twixt optimist and pessimist
     The difference is droll;
The optimist sees the doughnut,
     The pessimist, the hole.   McLANDBURGH WILSON

The optimist sees an opportunity in every calamity; a pessimist sees a calamity in every opportunity.

An optimist is a bridegroom planning how he will spend his next paycheck.

A few years back, Montana State had a bad football season, but the coach faced the new year optimistically: "We're sure to improve," he said. "We lost all ten games last season. This year we have only nine games scheduled."

De good Lawd send me troubles
     An' I got to wuk 'em out.
     But I look aroun' an' see
     There's trouble all about.
An' when I see my troubles
     I jes look up an' grin
To think of all the troubles
     Dat I ain't in.

A sportsman who takes a frying pan on a fishing trip is an optimist.

The optimist is often as wrong as the pessimist; but he is far happier.

A 100 percent optimist is a man who thinks the time will come when there will be no more wisecrack definitions of an optimist.

A 100 percent optimist is a man who believes the thinning out of his hair is only a temporary matter.

Optimism is man's passport to a better tomorrow.

Optimism is

> taking a camera along when you go fishing;
> the ability to smile at misfortune when fortune doesn't smile at you;
> expecting your wife to drive a car six feet wide through a garage doorway eight feet narrow;
> never worrying about the future because it never becomes serious until it is the present;
> the cheerful frame of mind that enables a teapot to sing, though it is in hot water up to its nose.

An optimist is a driver who thinks that the empty space at the curb won't have a hydrant beside it.

A man who keeps his motor running while waiting for a woman is an optimist.

Since the house is on fire let us warm ourselves.

ITALIAN PROVERB

An optimist is one who sends a package by parcel post and marks it "Rush!"

No one ever injured his eyesight by looking on the bright side of things.

An optimist believes that what's going to happen will be postponed.

An optimist is one who believes a change in the political regime will lower taxes. MAX GRALNICK

An optimist is anyone who expects change. JOHN J. PLOMP

The man who sees a green light everywhere is an optimist. ALBERT SCHWEITZER

An optimist is a man who hasn't gotten around to reading the morning papers. EARL WILSON

A man who gets treed by a lion but enjoys the scenery is an optimist. WALTER WINCHELL

Plans/Ideals

Don't lose sight of good planning and insight. Hang on to them, for they fill you with life and bring you honor and respect.

PROVERBS 3:21-22

We can make our plans, but the Lord determines our steps. Commit your work to the Lord, and then your plans will succeed. The Lord has made everything for his own purposes.

PROVERBS 16:9, 3-4

The plans of the godly are just; the advice of the wicked is treacherous.

PROVERBS 12:5

Plans/Ideals

To awake each morning with a smile brightening my face;
To greet the day with reverence for the opportunities it
　contains;
To approach my work with a clean mind;
To hold ever before me, even in the doing of the little things,
　the Ultimate Purpose toward which I am working;
To meet men and women with laughter on my lips and love in
　my heart;
To be gentle and kind, and courteous through all the hours;
To approach the night with weariness that ever woos sleep and
　the joy that comes from work well done—
This is how I desire to waste wisely my days.　　THOMAS DEKK

Long-range purposes keep you from being frustrated by
short-term failures.

Goals: write them down; hang them up; and with God's help,
watch them happen!

In the long run you hit only what you aim at. Therefore,
though you should fail immediately, you had better aim at
something high.　　HENRY DAVID THOREAU

Live your life each day as you would climb a mountain.

Ideals may be beyond our reach but never beyond our fondest
hopes.

Those who have a "why" to live, can bear with almost any
"how."　　VIKTOR FRANKL

If you are satisfied with yourself, you had better change your
ideals.

Clear definition of goals is the key to success.

EDISON MONTGOMERY

It's a sad fact that many politicians are more concerned about deals than ideals.

Keep your ideals high enough to inspire you and low enough to encourage you.

Prayer

The Lord is close to all who call on
him, yes, to all who call
on him sincerely.

PSALM 145:18

———

The Lord hates the sacrifice of the
wicked, but he delights in the prayers
of the upright. The Lord is far from
the wicked, but he hears the prayers
of the righteous.

PROVERBS 15:8, 29

———

Well, God doesn't listen to sinners,
but he is ready to hear those who
worship him and do his will.

JOHN 9:31

Prayer

In the morning, prayer is the key that opens to us the treasures of God's mercies and blessings; in the evening it is the key that shuts us up under his protection and safeguard.

The less I pray, the harder it gets; the more I pray, the better it goes.
MARTIN LUTHER

Prayer is the contemplation of the facts of life from the highest point of view.
RALPH WALDO EMERSON

Man is never so tall as when he kneels before God—never so great as when he humbles himself before God. And the man who kneels to God can stand up to anything.
LOUIS H. EVANS

Why Wonder
If radio's slim fingers
can pluck a melody
from the night and toss it over
a continent or sea;
If the petaled white notes
of a violin
are blown across a mountain
or a city's din;
If songs, like crimson roses
are culled from the thin blue air;
Why should mortals wonder
that God hears and answers prayer?
ETHEL ROMIG FULLER

Prayer doesn't get man's will done in heaven; it gets God's will done on earth.
RONALD DUNN

Lord, fill my mouth
With worthwhile stuff.
And nudge me when
I've said enough!

Prayer is exhaling the spirit of man and inhaling the Spirit of
God.   EDWIN KEITH

Prayerless pews make powerless pulpits.

Preacher: "Do you say your prayers at night, little boy?"
Jimmy: "Yes, sir."
Preacher: "Do you say your prayers in the morning, too?"
Jimmy: "No, sir. I ain't scared in the daytime."

It's a good idea to tune your instruments by prayer before the
concert of the day begins.

Let's move from theology to kneeology! Power for victory in
spiritual warfare is found in prayer.   ROBERT R. LAWRENCE

The quickest way to get back on your feet is to get down on
your knees.

Chin up, knees down.

Don't pray to escape trouble. Don't pray to be comfortable in
your emotions. Pray to do the will of God in every situation.
Nothing else is worth praying for.   SAMUEL M. SHOEMAKER

God does nothing but in answer to prayer.   JOHN WESLEY

I have found the greatest power in the world is the power of
prayer.   CECIL B. DeMILLE

I am better or worse as I pray more or less. It works for me
with mathematical precision.   E. STANLEY JONES

Prayer is not conquering God's reluctance, but taking hold of God's willingness.　　　　　　　　　PHILLIPS BROOKS

There are three answers to prayer: yes, no, and wait.

Prayerfulness begets carefulness.

Walk softly; speak tenderly; pray fervently.

A Sunday school teacher asked a little girl if she said her prayers every night.
"No, not every night," declared the child. "'Cause some nights I don't want anything."

We go down on our knees, or we go down to oblivion.

Prayer is not learned in the classroom but in the closet.　　　　　　　　　E. M. BOUNDS

Prayer is not merely an occasional impulse to which we respond when we are in trouble; prayer is a life attitude.　　　　　　　　　WALTER A. MUELLER

Pray when you don't feel like it; pray when you feel like it; pray until you feel like it.

Time spent on the knees in prayer will do more to remedy heart strain and nerve worry than anything else.　　　　　　　　　GEORGE DAVID STEWART

Prayer moves the hand which moves the world.　　　　　　　　　JOHN AIKMAN WALLACE

Overheard at bedtime prayers: "I'm not praying for anything for myself . . . just a new bike for my brother that we both can ride!"

Preparation

A prudent person foresees the danger
ahead and takes precautions;
the simpleton goes blindly on
and suffers the consequences.

PROVERBS 22:3

The horses are prepared for battle,
but the victory belongs to the Lord.

PROVERBS 21:31

Wisdom has built her spacious house
with seven pillars. She has prepared
a great banquet.

PROVERBS 9:1-2

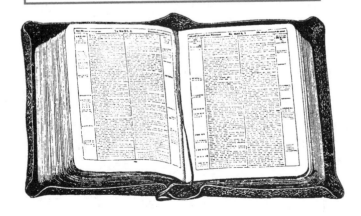

Preparation

He who doesn't know where he's going should not start his journey.

One of life's most painful moments comes when we must admit that we didn't do our homework, that we are not prepared.   MERLIN OLSON

Opportunity has the uncanny habit of favoring those who have paid the price of years of preparation.

Prepare and prevent instead of repair and repent.

When you're thirsty, it's too late to think about digging a well.

Make no little plans;
    They have no magic to stir
        men's blood
And probably themselves will not
        be realized.
Make big plans; aim high
        in hope of work,
Remembering that a noble,
        logical diagram
Once recorded will not die.   DAVID H. BURNHAM

The price of mastery in any field is thorough preparation.

I will study and get ready, and perhaps my chance will come.
                                            ABRAHAM LINCOLN

Make preparations in advance. You never have trouble if you are prepared for it.   THEODORE ROOSEVELT

Chance favors only the mind which is prepared. LOUIS PASTEUR

A danger foreseen is half avoided. THOMAS FULLER

A forewarned man is worth two. SPANISH PROVERB

Pride

If you have been a fool by being proud or plotting evil, don't brag about it—cover your mouth with your hand in shame.

PROVERBS 30:32

Pride leads to disgrace, but with humility comes wisdom.

PROVERBS 11:2

Pride goes before destruction, and haughtiness before a fall. It is better to live humbly with the poor than to share plunder with the proud.

PROVERBS 16:18-19

Pride

When a proud man hears another praised, he feels himself injured.   ENGLISH PROVERB

The core of pride is self-rejection.   ERIC HOFFER

Pride is the never-failing vice of fools.   ALEXANDER POPE

Pride is littleness.   WILLIAM WORDSWORTH

A big wheel is someone who runs around in circles.

Temper is what gets most of us in trouble. Pride keeps us there.

The best remedy for puffed-up pride is a pinprick.

People wrap themselves up in the flimsy garments of their own righteousness and then complain of the cold.

When a man is wrapped up in himself, he makes a pretty small package.   JOHN RUSKIN

He who pats himself on the back may dislocate his shoulder.

If he could only see how small a vacancy his death would leave, the proud man would think less of the place he occupies in his lifetime.   ERNEST LEGOUVÉ

Some folks are as proud of their ancestors as if they were responsible for them.

Always hold your head up, but be careful to keep your nose at a friendly level.

Don't let your pride become inflated—you may have to swallow it someday.

Nothing pleases a small man more than an opportunity to crack a big whip.

Many a bee has been drowned in his own honey.

Proud people are always letting off esteem.

Priorities

In everything you do, put God first,
and he will direct you and crown your
efforts with success.

PROVERBS 3:6, TLB

———

He will give you all you need from
day to day if you live for him and
make the Kingdom of God your
primary concern.

MATTHEW 6:33

———

Honor the Lord with your wealth and
with the best part of everything your
land produces. Then he will fill your
barns with grain, and your vats will
overflow with the finest wine.

PROVERBS 3:9-10

Priorities

He who asks a question may be a fool for five minutes; he who never asks a question remains a fool forever.

Do not have your concert first and tune your instruments afterward. Begin the day with God.   JAMES H. TAYLOR

Show me the way
Not to fortune and fame,
Not how to win laurels
Or praise for my name—
But show me the way
To spread "The Great Story"
That Thine is The Kingdom
And Power and Glory.   HELEN STEINER RICE

Asking saves a lot of guesswork.

People who want to move mountains must start by carrying away small stones.

Only one life, 'twill soon be past.
Only what's done for Christ will last.

Taking first things first often reduces the most complex human problem to a manageable proportion.
                   DWIGHT D. EISENHOWER

We are silent at the beginning of the day because God should have the first word, and we are silent before going to sleep because the last word also belongs to God.
                   DIETRICH BONHOEFFER

Quarrels

As the beating of cream yields butter, and a blow to the nose causes bleeding, so anger causes quarrels.

PROVERBS 30:33

Throw out the mocker, and fighting, quarrels, and insults will disappear.

PROVERBS 22:10

Avoiding a fight is a mark of honor; only fools insist on quarreling.

PROVERBS 20:3

Beginning a quarrel is like opening a floodgate, so drop the matter before a dispute breaks out. Anyone who loves to quarrel loves sin; anyone who speaks boastfully invites disaster.

PROVERBS 17:14, 19

Quarrels

In quarreling, the truth is always lost.   PUBLIUS SYRUS

When one word leads to another, it generally ends up in a quarrel, a speech, or a dictionary.

Very often a fight for what is right turns into a quarrel for what is left.

It takes two to make a quarrel, but only one to end it.
                                                        SPANISH PROVERB

Some husbands quarrel with their wives, and others have learned to say, "Yes, dear."

Husband, during quarrel: "You talk like an idiot!"
Wife: "I have to talk so you can understand me!"

It takes two to make a quarrel, but one gets the blame.

Two things would prevent many quarrels: First, making sure we are disputing about terms rather than facts. Second, examining whether the difference of opinion is worth contending about.

One of the little-mentioned but considerable advantages of rural living is that family quarrels can't be overheard.
                                                        SYDNEY HARRIS

Next to the wound, what women make best is the bandage.
                                                        BARBEY D'AUREVILLY

Reputation

Never let loyalty and kindness get away from you! Wear them like a necklace; write them deep within your heart. Then you will find favor with both God and people, and you will gain a good reputation.

PROVERBS 3:3-4

———

Choose a good reputation over great riches, for being held in high esteem is better than having silver or gold.

PROVERBS 22:1

Reputation

The circumstances amid which you live determine your reputation; the truth you believe determines your character.

Reputation is what you are supposed to be; character is what you are.

Reputation is the photograph, character is the face.

Reputation comes over one from without; character grows up from within.

Reputation is what you have when you come to a new community; character is what you have when you go away.

Your reputation is learned in an hour; your character does not come to light for a year.

Reputation grows like a mushroom; character grows like the oak.

A single newspaper report gives you your reputation; a life of toil gives you your character.

Reputation makes you rich or poor; character makes you happy or miserable.

It's what you do when you have nothing to do that reveals what you are.

Reputation is what you need to get a job; character is what you need to keep it.

White lies are likely to leave black marks on a man's reputation.

A man has three names: the name he inherits, the name his parents give him, and the name he makes for himself.

No one can build a reputation on what he plans for tomorrow.

It's easier to acquire a good reputation than to lose a bad one.

A reputation may be repaired, but people always keep their eyes on the place where the crack is.

Judge a man by the reputation of his enemies.
ARABIC PROVERB

Glass, china, and reputation are easily crack'd and never well mended. BENJAMIN FRANKLIN

The slanderer differs from the assassin only in that he murders the reputation instead of the body.

No man is rich enough to buy back his past.

Many men would turn over a new leaf if they could tear out some of the old pages.

Family Name
You got it from your father,
It was all he had to give.
So it's yours to use and cherish,
For as long as you may live.

If you lose the watch he gave you,
It can always be replaced.
But a black mark on your name, son,
Can never be erased.

It was clean the day you took it,
And a worthy name to bear.
When he got it from his father,
There was no dishonor there.

So make sure you guard it wisely,
After all is said and done.
You'll be glad the name is spotless,
When you give it to your son.   AUTHOR UNKNOWN

Everyone should fear death until he has something that will
live on after his death.

The best inheritance parents can leave a child is a good name.

Responsibility

It is poor judgment to co-sign a friend's note, to become responsible for a neighbor's debts.

PROVERBS 17:18

Here is my final conclusion: Fear God and obey his commands, for this is the duty of every person.

ECCLESIASTES 12:13

Rescue those who are unjustly sentenced to death; don't stand back and let them die. Don't try to avoid responsibility by saying you didn't know about it. For God knows all hearts, and he sees you. He keeps watch over your soul, and he knows you knew! And he will judge all people according to what they have done.

PROVERBS 24:11-12

Responsibility

When your shoulders are carrying a load of responsibility, there isn't room for chips.

You can't escape the responsibility of tomorrow by evading it today. ABRAHAM LINCOLN

The buck stops here. HARRY S. TRUMAN

Admission: I have a very responsible job here; I'm responsible for everything that goes wrong.

Man blames most accidents on fate—but feels personally responsible when he scores a hole in one.

Some men grow under responsibility, while others only swell.

The price of greatness is responsibility. WINSTON CHURCHILL

Privilege and responsibility are two sides of the same coin.

He who buries his talent is making a grave mistake.

The ability to accept responsibility is the measure of the man. ROY L. SMITH

You cannot help men permanently by doing for them what they could and should do for themselves. ABRAHAM LINCOLN

Responsibility is my response to God's ability. ALBERT J. LOWN

It's an awesome responsibility to own a Bible.

Some people recognize their responsibilities in time to dodge them.

Riches

Choose a good reputation over great riches, for being held in high esteem is better than having silver or gold. True humility and fear of the Lord lead to riches, honor, and long life.

PROVERBS 22:1, 4

———

Riches won't help on the day of judgment. Evil people get rich for the moment, but the reward of the godly will last. It is possible to give freely and become more wealthy, but those who are stingy will lose everything.

PROVERBS 11:4, 18, 24

———

Honor the Lord with your wealth and with the best part of everything your land produces.

PROVERBS 3:9

Riches

People who spend too much time worrying about their station in life will often be told where to get off.

You can dial for the weather,
   For the time and for prayers,
For Dow Jones reports on
   Most widely held shares,
For horoscopes, even
   For jokes and good health.
I wish I could get
   The number for wealth.
                      BERT H. KRUSE

No good man became suddenly rich.   PUBLIUS SYRUS

My riches consist not in the extent of my possessions but in the fewness of my wants.   J. BROTHERTON

Few rich men own their own property. The property owns them.   ROBERT INGERSOLL

To be content with what we possess is the greatest and most secure of riches.   CICERO

Riches are not an end of life but an instrument of life.
                  HENRY WARD BEECHER

Make no mistake, my friend, it takes more than money to make men rich.   A. P. GOUTHEY

The wretchedness of being rich is that you live with rich people.   LOGAN PEARSALL SMITH

Better see rightly on a pound a week than squint on a million.
GEORGE BERNARD SHAW

I find all this money a considerable burden.
JOHN PAUL GETTY JR.

Life begets life. Energy creates energy. It is by spending oneself that one becomes rich.　　　　　SARAH BERNHARDT

Abundance, unless we use the utmost care, destroys discipline.

A poor man who marries a wealthy woman gets a ruler and not a wife.

Great wealth and contentment seldom live together.

Self-Centeredness

There is more hope for fools than for
people who think they are wise.

PROVERBS 26:12

─────

Don't praise yourself; let others do it!

PROVERBS 27:2

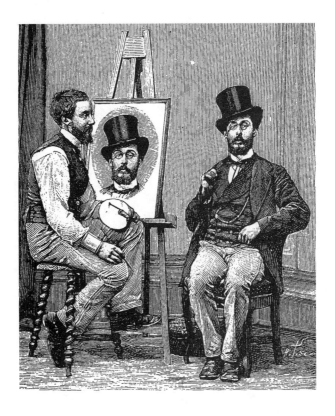

Self-Centeredness

Conceit is an odd disease; it makes everybody sick but the one who has it.

The last time I saw him he was walking down Lover's Lane holding his own hand. FRED ALLEN

He who falls in love with himself will have no rivals.

He who is full of himself is likely to be quite empty.

Talk to a man about himself and he will listen for hours. BENJAMIN DISRAELI

Conceit is the quicksand of success. ARNOLD H. GLASSGOW

A conceited man has a swelling head and a shrinking brain.

Conceit is the most incurable disease that is known to the human soul. HENRY WARD BEECHER

A conceited man is satisfied with the effect he produces on himself. MAX BEERBOHM

An egotist is me-deep in conversation. WILLIAM BERTOLOTT

A self-made man who worships his creator is an egotist. JOHN BRIGHT

An egotist is a cock who thinks the sun has risen to hear him crow. GEORGE ELIOT

The egotist's only good feature is that he seldom gossips about other people.

He who sings his own praises seldom gets the right pitch.

Egotism: I strain.

Silence

> Even fools are thought to be wise
> when they keep silent; when they keep
> their mouths shut, they seem
> intelligent.
>
> PROVERBS 17:28

Silence

He who is a man of silence is a man of sense.

Some people won't suffer in silence because that would take the pleasure out of it.

Wisdom is made up of ten parts, nine of which are silence—the tenth, brevity.

It is better to be silent and be considered a fool than to speak and remove all doubt.   ABRAHAM LINCOLN

It doesn't do to do much talking when
    You're mad enough to choke,
For the word that hits the hardest is
    The one that's never spoke.
Let the other fellow do the talking
    Till the storm has rolled away,
Then he'll do a heap of thinking 'bout
    The things you didn't say.

You must speak up to be heard, but sometimes you have to shut up to be appreciated.

If there's a substitute for brains, it has to be silence.

Talking comes by nature; silence by wisdom.

In silence man can most readily preserve his integrity.
                                                    MEISTER WICKHART

If you rest your chin in your hands when you think, it will keep your mouth shut so you won't disturb yourself.

Silence isolates us from the crowds that love to pool their misery; an unhappy civilization is always gregarious.

BISHOP FULTON J. SHEEN

Luigi Tarisio was found dead one morning with scarcely a comfort in his home but with 246 violins crammed into his attic, the best violins in the bottom drawer of an old rickety bureau. This man's devotion to the violin robbed the world of the beautiful music his treasured violins could have produced. Because of Luigi and others like him, by the time the greatest Stradivarius was first played it had 147 silent years.

In Maine, we have a saying that there's no point in speaking unless you can improve on silence.   EDMUND MUSKIE

Discretion is putting two and two together and keeping your mouth shut.

At no time is it easier to keep your mouth shut than during an audit of your income-tax return.

Silence is the best and surest way to hide ignorance.

Be silent or let thy words be worth more than silence.

PYTHAGORAS

Silence is the voice of the convinced; loudness is the voice of those who want to convince themselves.   DAGOBERT RUNES

Silence at the proper season is wisdom, and better than any speech.   PLUTARCH

The wisest retort is often silence.   ORLANDO WRIGHT

Silence is one of the hardest things to refute.   JOSH BILLINGS

There are three times when you should never say anything important to a person: when he is tired, when he is angry, and when he has just made a mistake.

A man is known by the silence he keeps.

People who can hold their tongues rarely have any trouble holding their friends.

If you don't say anything, you won't be called on to repeat it.

CALVIN COOLIDGE

The hardest thing to keep is quiet!

Sticks and stones are hard on bones.
   Aimed with angry art,
Words can sting like anything
   But silence breaks the heart.   PHYLLIS MCGINLEY

It's funny how people on a diet are never reduced to silence.

A wise man is one who has an open mind and a closed mouth.

If you keep your mouth shut, you won't put your foot in it.

None preaches better than the ant, and she says nothing.

BENJAMIN FRANKLIN

Silence, along with modesty, is a great aid to conversation.

MICHEL DE MONTAIGNE

No one has ever repented of having held his tongue.

A closed mouth catches no flies.

True silence is the rest of the mind.   WILLIAM PENN

Sincerity

Who may worship in
your sanctuary, Lord?
Who may enter your presence
on your holy hill?

Those who lead blameless lives
and do what is right,
speaking the truth from
sincere hearts.

PSALM 15:1-2

———

Fear the Lord and serve Him in
sincerity and truth.

JOSHUA 24:14, NASB

Sincerity

Sincerity: to practice more than your tongue says.

A blush is one thing that can't be counterfeited.

Sincerity—a silent address. OLIVER GOLDSMITH

Sincerity makes the least man to be of more value than the most talented hypocrite. CHARLES SPURGEON

Sincerity: being yourself in any direction.

The primary condition for being sincere is the same as for being humble: not to boast about it, and probably not even to be aware of it. HENRI PEYRE

I want to see you shoot the way you shout. THEODORE ROOSEVELT

Insincere praise is worse than no praise at all.

The only guide to a man is his conscience; the only shield to his memory is the rectitude and sincerity of his actions. WINSTON CHURCHILL

Sincerity is the face of the soul.

The trouble with being sincere is that people will be inclined to think you're just putting on an act.

A hypocrite never intends to be what he pretends to be.

Be suspicious of your sincerity when you are the advocate of that upon which your livelihood depends. JOHN LANCASTER SPALDING

241

Sincerity needs no witnesses.

Prayer must mean something to us if it is to mean anything to God.

When leading a public prayer, speak loudly enough to be heard of men and sincerely enough to be heard of God.

The most important thing in politics is sincerity, whether you mean it or not.

We are not sent into the world to do anything into which we cannot put our hearts. JOHN RUSKIN

What is uttered from the heart alone
Will win the hearts of others to your own. GOETHE

The devil is sincere, but he is sincerely wrong. BILLY GRAHAM

Be sincere with your compliments. Most people can tell the difference between sugar and saccharine.

The sincere man suspects that he, too, is sometimes guilty of the faults he sees in others.

False doctrine is not right just because a person sincerely believes it.

Of all the evil spirits abroad at this hour in the world, insincerity is the most dangerous. JAMES ANTHONY FROUDE

Sincerity—an openness of heart.
FRANÇOIS DE LA ROCHEFOUCAULD

I should say sincerity, a deep, great genuine sincerity, is the characteristic of all men in any way heroic. THOMAS CARLYLE

The professional politician can sympathize with the professional advertiser. Both must resign themselves to a low public estimation of their veracity and sincerity. ENOCH POWELL

A little sincerity is a dangerous thing, and a great deal is absolutely fatal. OSCAR WILDE

Smiles

A glad heart makes a happy face; a
broken heart crushes the spirit.

PROVERBS 15:13

When the king smiles, there is life;
his favor refreshes like a gentle rain.

PROVERBS 16:15

Smiles

The curve of a smile can set a lot of things straight.

A warm smile thaws an icy stare.

All people smile in the same language.

Why not wear a smile? It's just about the only thing you can wear that isn't taxed.

A smile is God's cosmetic.

A smile is the lighting system of the face and the heating system of the heart.

When you see someone without a smile, give him one of yours.

A smile is a wrinkle that shouldn't be removed.

The person who does not have a smiling face should not open his shop.

What sunshine is to flowers, smiles are to humanity.

JOSEPH ADDISON

Smile—it improves your face value.

Smile—it's the second best thing you can do with your lips.

Before you put on a frown, my friend, make absolutely certain there are no smiles available.

Wear a smile and have friends; wear a scowl and have wrinkles.

A smile is the universal welcome. MAX EASTMAN

The world always looks brighter from behind a smile.

A laugh is a smile that bursts. MARY WALDRIP

'Tis easy enough to be pleasant,
    When life flows along like a song;
But the man worthwhile is the one who will smile
    When everything goes dead wrong.   ELLA WHEELER WILCOX

You're never fully dressed without a smile.   MARTIN CHARNIN

It takes seventeen muscles to smile and forty-three to frown.

All the statistics in the world can't measure the warmth of a
smile. CHRIS HART

No matter how grouchy you're feeling,
    You'll find the smile more or less healing.
      It grows in a wreath
      All around the front teeth—
Thus preserving the face from congealing.   ANTHONY EUWER

A smile confuses an approaching frown.

If I can make people smile, then I have served my purpose for
God. RED SKELTON

A smile is an inexpensive way to improve your looks.
CHARLES GORDY

Wrinkles should merely indicate where the smiles have been.
MARK TWAIN

If you didn't start out the day with a smile, it's not too late to start practicing for tomorrow.

Laughter is regional: a smile extends over the whole face.

MALCOLM DE CHAZAL

If you'd like to spoil the day for a grouch, give him a smile.

If you can smile when all else is going wrong, you must be a plumber working for triple time on a Sunday.

A smile costs nothing but gives much. It enriches those who receive without making poorer those who give. It takes but a moment, but the memory of it sometimes lasts forever. None is so rich or mighty that he can get along without it, and none is so poor that he cannot be made rich by it. A smile creates happiness in the home, fosters goodwill in business and is the countersign of friendship. It brings rest to the weary, cheer to the discouraged, sunshine to the sad, and is nature's best antidote for trouble. Yet it cannot be bought, begged, borrowed, or stolen, for it is something that is of no value to anyone until it is given away. Some people are too tired to give you a smile. Give them one of yours, as none needs a smile so much as he who has no more to give.

Keep smiling—it makes people wonder what you've been up to.

The bitterest misfortune can be covered up with a smile.

YIDDISH PROVERB

There are no language barriers when you are smiling.

ALLEN KLEIN

A smile is a powerful weapon; you can even break ice with it.

Smiles reach the hard-to-reach places.   STEVE WILSON

A smile is a passport that will take you anywhere you want to go.

The fruit of love is service. The fruit of service is peace. And peace begins with a smile.   MOTHER TERESA

Speech/Speaker

Wise speech is rarer and more
valuable than gold and rubies.
Anyone who loves a pure heart and
gracious speech is the king's friend.

PROVERBS 20:15; 22:11

The king is pleased with righteous
lips; he loves those who speak
honestly. From a wise mind comes
wise speech. My child, how I will
rejoice if you become wise. Yes, my
heart will thrill when you speak what
is right and just.

PROVERBS 16:13, 23; 23:15-16

Patience can persuade a prince,
and soft speech can crush
strong opposition.

PROVERBS 25:15

Speech/Speaker

A perfect after-dinner speech is the shortest distance between two jokes.

Politician: "Have you heard my last speech?"
Voter: "I hope so!"

It's not always what you say but the way you say it.

Wife: "Don't be so impolite. You've yawned five times while I've been talking to you."
Husband: "I wasn't yawning. I was trying to say something!"

A good speech consists of a good beginning and a good ending, preferably close together.

Too many speakers need no introduction, just a conclusion.

Adam was created first—to give him a chance to say something.

Most girls have a speech impediment: they have to stop to breathe!

As a vessel is known by its sound whether it be cracked or not, so men are proved by their speeches whether they be wise or foolish.
                                                    DEMOSTHENES

The best ingredient in the recipe for public speaking is the shortening.

Oratory: the art of making deep noises from the chest sound like important messages from the brain.

In making a good speech, it is all right to have a train of thought just as long as you make sure you also have a terminal.

Be careful what you say around children. They are like blotters: They soak it all in and get it all backward.

Speeches are like babies—easy to conceive but hard to deliver.

PAT O'MALLEY

There are two things that are more difficult than making an after-dinner speech: climbing a wall which is leaning toward you and kissing a girl who is leaning away from you.

WINSTON CHURCHILL

The things I say and do today
In memory's book, I'll keep,
And when I'm old and read them—
Will I laugh or will I weep?

Most politicians don't bore people with long speeches; they do it with short ones.

It usually takes me more than three weeks to prepare a good impromptu speech. MARK TWAIN

Let us give thanks that we live in a free country where a man can say what he thinks if he isn't afraid of his wife, his neighbors, or his boss, and if he's sure it won't hurt his business.

Nothing is often a very good thing to say.

Public speaking is the art of diluting a two-minute idea with a two-hour vocabulary.

The ability to speak several languages is valuable, but the art of keeping silent in one is precious.

251

After a speaker had talked loud and long, he asked the audience if there were any questions. A hand shot up. The speaker nodded. "What time is it?" the listener inquired.

If you haven't struck oil in your first three minutes, stop boring.   GEORGE JESSEL

I disapprove of what you say, but I will defend to the death your right to say it.   VOLTAIRE

If your mind goes blank, be sure to turn off the sound.

Success

People who cover over their sins will not prosper. But if they confess and forsake them, they will receive mercy.

PROVERBS 28:13

The whole city celebrates when the godly succeed; they shout for joy when the godless die.

PROVERBS 11:10

Commit your work to the Lord, and then your plans will succeed.

PROVERBS 16:3

Success

You don't have to lie awake nights to succeed—just stay awake days.

Accept the challenges, so that you may feel the exhilaration of victory. GEORGE S. PATTON

Lincoln's road to the White House:

> Failed in business in 1831
> Defeated for legislature in 1832
> Second failure in business in 1833
> Suffered a nervous breakdown in 1836
> Defeated for speaker in 1838
> Defeated for elector in 1840
> Defeated for Congress in 1843
> Defeated for Senate in 1855
> Defeated for vice president in 1856
> Defeated for Senate in 1858
> Elected president in 1860

The *Los Angeles Times* described a Beverly Hills barber's career as a case of "climbing the lather of success."

If at first you don't succeed, avoid skydiving.

Recipe for success: Study while others are sleeping; work while others are loafing; prepare while others are playing; and dream while others are wishing. WILLIAM A. WARD

Success is the child of audacity. BENJAMIN DISRAELI

Success often comes from taking a misstep in the right direction.

If at first you don't succeed, you're running about average.

It takes twenty years to make an overnight success.

EDDIE CANTOR

You have reached the pinnacle of success as soon as you become uninterested in money, compliments or publicity.

EDDIE RICKENBACKER

He who wakes up and finds himself successful has not been asleep.

President Schwab of Bethlehem Steel said that success was 10 percent ability, 10 percent appearance, 5 percent availability, 5 percent adaptability, and 70 percent attitude.

If you want to be successful, it's just this simple: Know what you're doing. Love what you're doing. And believe in what you're doing.

O. A. BATTISTA

The man is a success who has lived well, laughed often and loved much; who has gained the respect of intelligent men and the love of children; who has filled his niche and accomplished his task; who leaves the world better than he found it, whether by an improved poppy, a perfect poem or a rescued soul; who never lacked appreciation of earth's beauty or failed to express it; who looked for the best in others and gave the best he had.

ROBERT LOUIS STEVENSON

All the roads to success are uphill.

It's not a successful climb unless you enjoy the journey.

DAN BENSON

You will find the key to success under the alarm clock.

There are no secrets to success. It is the result of preparation, hard work, and learning from failure. COLIN L. POWELL

Success is never final and failure never fatal. It's courage that counts. GEORGE TILTON

A lot of people owe their success to advice they didn't take.

The father of success is work—the mother of achievement is ambition.

A man rarely succeeds at anything unless he has fun doing it.

Success is to be measured not so much by the position that one has reached in life as by the obstacles which he has overcome while trying to succeed. BOOKER T. WASHINGTON

Success is simply a matter of luck. Ask any failure. EARL WILSON

Success consists of getting up just one more time than you fall.
OLIVER GOLDSMITH

Success covers a multitude of blunders. GEORGE BERNARD SHAW

The toughest thing about success is that you've got to keep on being successful. IRVING BERLIN

Women are rarely as successful as men—they have no wives to advise them.

Elbow grease is still the best lubricant for success.

Success has many friends. GREEK PROVERB

Tact

Trusting oneself is foolish, but those
who walk in wisdom are safe.

PROVERBS 28:26

———

Pay attention to my wisdom; listen
carefully to my wise counsel. Then
you will learn to be discreet and will
store up knowledge.

PROVERBS 5:1-2

———

A wise man is mightier than a strong
man, and a man of knowledge is more
powerful than a strong man.

PROVERBS 24:5

Tact

Tact is changing the subject without changing your mind.

A diplomat can keep his shirt on while getting something off his chest.

Silence is not always tact, and it is tact that is golden, not silence. SAMUEL BUTLER

A tactful husband said to his wife, "How do you expect me to remember your birthday when you never look any older?"

Diplomacy is the art of taking sides without anyone's knowing it.

You never know till you try to reach them how accessible men are; but you must approach each man by the right door. HENRY WARD BEECHER

Being diplomatic is telling your boss he has an open mind instead of telling him he has a hole in his head.

If you can pat a guy on the head when you feel like bashing it in, you're a diplomat.

A smile is the magic language of diplomacy that even a baby can understand.

Tact comes as much from goodness of heart as from fineness of taste. ENDYMION

A diplomat is a parent with two boys on different Little League teams.

Tact is the ability to describe others as they see themselves.

ABRAHAM LINCOLN

A tactful man remembers a lady's birthday but forgets her age.

Diplomacy is the art of saying, "Nice doggie!" until you can find a stick.

In order to be a diplomat one must speak a number of languages, including double-talk.

CAREY MCWILLIAMS

Diplomacy: The art of jumping into troubled waters without making a splash.

ART LINKLETTER

Talent is something, but tact is everything. Talent is serious, sober, grave and respectable; tact is all that, and more too. It is not a seventh sense, but it is the life of all the five. It is the open eye, the quick ear, the judging taste, the keen smell, and the lively touch; it is the interpreter of all riddles, the surmounter of all difficulties, the remover of all obstacles.

W. P. SCARGILL

Diplomacy is cutting the other fellow's throat without using a knife.

Let us never negotiate out of fear, but let us never fear to negotiate.

JOHN F. KENNEDY

Diplomacy is the art of letting someone else have your way.

Tact is the ability to change a porcupine into an opossum.

Diplomacy is the art of turning a dropped stitch into a loophole.

Diplomacy is the ability to put your best foot forward without stepping on anybody's toes.

A diplomat is a person who thinks twice before saying nothing.

Tact is knowing how far to go before going too far.

Diplomats should emulate musicians who never conduct foreign overtures without knowing the score.

When a diplomat says yes, he means perhaps; when he says perhaps, he means no; when he says no, he is no diplomat.

Lacking in tact, the young man looked at the high prices on the menu, turned to his date, and said: "What will you have, my plump little doll?"

A fellow who prefers ironing out his differences to flattening his opponent is a diplomat.

A man with diplomacy convinces his wife that a woman looks stout in a fur coat.

A person who can be disarming even though his country isn't is a diplomat.

A diplomat is a man who can juggle a hot potato long enough for it to become a cold issue.

Do not use a hatchet to remove a fly from your friend's forehead.

The nearer you come in relation with a person, the more necessary do tact and courtesy become. OLIVER WENDELL HOLMES

The best way to knock the chip off your neighbor's shoulder is to pat him on the back.

Social tact is making your guests feel at home, even though you wish they were.

People with tact have less to retract.

An unwise man tells a woman to stop talking so much, but a tactful man tells her that her mouth is extremely beautiful when her lips are closed.

Tact is the ability to make a person see the lightning without letting him feel the bolt.

Teamwork

The one who plants and the one who waters work as a team with the same purpose. Yet they will be rewarded individually, according to their own hard work.

1 CORINTHIANS 3:8-9

A kingdom at war with itself will collapse. A home divided against itself is doomed.

JESUS, MARK 3:24-25

Teamwork

Let's remember that it takes both the white and the black keys of the piano to play "The Star-Spangled Banner."

A little boy was playing all alone in the front yard when a neighbor came along and asked where his brother was. "Oh," he said, "he's in the house playing a duet. I finished first."

You've got to have the blocking or you can't gain the yards.

JOE PERRY

United we stand; divided we fall.

AESOP

Teamwork is a joint action whose advantage is that there is always someone you can blame if things go wrong.

A bundle of sticks is always stronger than a single twig.

Light is the task when many share the toil.

HOMER

A lot of people are lonely because they build walls instead of bridges.

If you don't believe in cooperation, look what happens when a car loses one of its wheels.

One lights the fire; the other fans it.

You cannot sink someone else's end of the boat and still keep your own afloat.

CHARLES BOWER

All your strength is in union. All your danger is in discord.

HENRY WADSWORTH LONGFELLOW

Temper

Those who are short-tempered do foolish things, and schemers are hated.

PROVERBS 14:17

———

It is better to be patient than powerful; it is better to have self-control than to conquer a city.

PROVERBS 16:32

———

A person without self-control is as defenseless as a city with broken-down walls.

PROVERBS 25:28

Temper

You are not a dynamic person simply because you blow your top.

People who fly into a rage usually make a bad landing.

The best time to keep your shirt on is when you're hot under the collar.

He who loses his temper should not look for it.

Nothing will cook your goose faster than a boiling-hot temper.

He who loses his temper usually loses.

To stay out of hot water, keep a cool head.

Poise is the act of raising your eyebrows instead of the roof.

Funny thing about temper: You can't get rid of it by losing it.

The world needs more warm hearts and fewer hotheads.

The emptier the pot, the quicker the boil—watch your temper!

Today's temper tantrum is tomorrow's antiestablishment demonstration.

When a man loses his temper, his reason goes on vacation.

Hitting the ceiling is the wrong way to get up in the world.

Time

Teach us to make the most of our time, so that we may grow in wisdom.

PSALM 90:12

Hard work means prosperity; only fools idle away their time.

PROVERBS 12:11

Young man, it's wonderful to be young! Enjoy every minute of it. Do everything you want to do; take it all in. But remember that you must give an account to God for everything you do.

ECCLESIASTES 11:9

Time

If you must kill time, work it to death.

He who kills time injures eternity.

> Take time to think—it is the source of power.
> Take time to play—it is the secret of perpetual youth.
> Take time to read—it is the fountain of wisdom.
> Take time to pray—it is the greatest power on earth.
> Take time to love and be loved—it is a God-given
>   privilege.
> Take time to be friendly—it is the road to happiness.
> Take time to laugh—it is the music of the soul.
> Take time to give—it is too short a day to be selfish.
> Take time to work—it is the price of success.

Time is a versatile performer. It flies, marches on, heals all wounds, runs out, and will tell.   FRANKLIN P. JONES

Why is there never enough time to do it right—but always enough time to do it over?

One thing you can learn by watching the clock is that it passes the time by keeping its hands busy.

When God wants to grow a squash He grows it one summer; but when He wants to grow an oak He takes a century.
                                                    JAMES A. GARFIELD

Our days are identical suitcases—all the same size—but some people can pack more into them than others.

No matter how hard you try to improve Mother Nature, you're not kidding Father Time. What Mother Nature giveth, Father Time taketh away.

Togetherness

How wonderful it is, how pleasant,
when brothers live together in
harmony!

PSALM 133:1

———

There are six things the Lord
hates—no, seven things he detests:
haughty eyes, a lying tongue, hands
that kill the innocent, a heart that
plots evil, feet that race to do wrong,
a false witness who pours out lies, a
person who sows discord among
brothers.

PROVERBS 6:16-19

———

Can two people walk together without
agreeing on the direction?

AMOS 3:3

Togetherness

Cooperation will solve many problems. Even freckles would form a nice tan if they would ever get together.

When we think of how no two snowflakes are alike, we find it inspiring that they work so well together on such joint projects as closing schools and making roads impassable.

My biggest thrill came the night Elgin Baylor and I combined for seventy-three points in Madison Square Garden. Elgin had seventy-one of them.   ROD HUNDLEY

Cooperation is doing with a smile what you have to do anyway.

Build for your team a feeling of oneness, of depending on one another and of strength to be derived by unity. VINCE LOMBARDI

We may not always see eye to eye, but we should walk hand in hand.

When two men in a business always agree, one of them is unnecessary.

The village band finished a vigorous and not overly harmonious selection. As the perspiring musicians sank to their seats after acknowledging the applause, the trombonist asked, "What's the next number?"
The leader replied, "'The Washington Post March.'"
"Oh no," gasped the trombonist. "I just got through playing that!"

It takes two hands to applaud.

Trouble

An unreliable messenger stumbles
into trouble, but a reliable messenger
brings healing.

PROVERBS 13:17

———

There is treasure in the house of the
godly, but the earnings of the wicked
bring trouble.

PROVERBS 15:6

———

If you keep your mouth shut, you will
stay out of trouble.

PROVERBS 21:23

Trouble

He who talks without thinking runs more risks than he who thinks without talking.

Troubles, like babies, grow larger with nursing.

When I go to bed, I leave my troubles in my clothes.
DUTCH PROVERB

Trouble—one product in which the supply exceeds the demand.

Troubles are tools by which God fashions us for better things.
HENRY WARD BEECHER

Nothing improves our prayer life faster than big troubles.

A kind word picks up a man when trouble weighs him down.

A lie is a coward's way of getting out of trouble.

The trouble with being a father is that by the time you're experienced, you're unemployable.

Adam may have had his troubles, but at least he didn't have to listen to Eve talk about the man she could have married.

When trouble moves in, make it pay the rent.

When the shepherd speaks well of the wolf, the sheep are in trouble.

If nobody knows the trouble you've seen, you don't live in a small town.

Trust

Trust in the Lord with all your heart;
do not depend on your own
understanding.

PROVERBS 3:5

———

Trust your money and down you go!
But the godly flourish like leaves
in spring.

PROVERBS 11:28

———

Those who listen to instruction will
prosper; those who trust the Lord will
be happy.

PROVERBS 16:20

———

Trusting oneself is foolish, but those
who walk in wisdom are safe.

PROVERBS 28:26

———

Fearing people is a dangerous trap,
but to trust the Lord means safety.

PROVERBS 29:25

Trust

Love all, trust a few.   WILLIAM SHAKESPEARE

In God we trust. All others pay cash.

Trust in God, and keep your powder dry.   OLIVER CROMWELL

All I have seen teaches me to trust the Creator for all I have
not seen.   RALPH WALDO EMERSON

He who cannot mind his own business should not be trusted
with the king's.

Trust, like fine china, once broken can be repaired, but it is
never quite the same.

The man who trusts God is the man who can be trusted.

Trust in yourself and you are doomed to disappointment;
trust in your friends and they will die and leave you; trust in
money and you may have it taken from you; trust in reputation and some slanderous tongue may blast it; but trust in
God, and you are never to be confounded in time or eternity.
                                           D. L. MOODY

As contagion of sickness makes sickness, contagion of trust
makes trust.   MARIANNE MOORE

To be trusted is a greater compliment than to be loved.
                                           J. MACDONALD

Trust in God does not supersede the employment of prudent
means on our part. To expect God's protection while we do
nothing is not to honor but to tempt providence.   QUESNEL

Trust men and they will be true to you; treat them greatly and they will show themselves great.   RALPH WALDO EMERSON

Trust him little who praises all, him less who censures all, and him least who is indifferent about all.   LAVATER

When you cannot trust God, you cannot trust anything; and when you cannot trust anything you get the condition of the world as it is today.   BASIL KING

He who trusts his own heart is a fool.

When a train goes through a tunnel and it gets dark, you don't throw away the ticket and jump off. You sit still and trust the engineer.   CORRIE TEN BOOM

Trust God for the unexpected, and let him surprise you by doing the unexplainable.

To him you tell your secrets, to him you resign your liberty.   SPANISH PROVERB

He who mistrusts most should be trusted least.   GREEK PROVERB

Understanding

Cry out for insight and understanding. Search for them as you would for lost money or hidden treasure.

PROVERBS 2:3-4

―――

The wise are known for their understanding, and instruction is appreciated if it's well presented.

PROVERBS 16:21

―――

To acquire wisdom is to love oneself; people who cherish understanding will prosper.

PROVERBS 19:8

Understanding

Husband's admission: "All right, you don't understand me. I don't suppose Mrs. Einstein understood Albert either."

The best way to be understood is to be understanding.

Sandy Koufax, star Dodger pitcher, discussing Coach Casey Stengel: "When I was young and smart, I couldn't understand him. Now that I am older and dumber, he makes sense to me."

Understanding is the reward of faith.   SAINT AUGUSTINE

Humanity's greatest need is not for more money but for more understanding.

If I knew you and you knew me,
    If both of us could clearly see,
And with an inner sight divine
    The meaning of your heart and mine,
I'm sure that we would differ less,
    And clasp our hands in friendliness;
Our thoughts would pleasantly agree
    If I knew you and you knew me.   NIXON WATERMAN

Let us have faith that right makes right; and in that faith let us to the end dare to do our duty as we understand it.
                                        ABRAHAM LINCOLN

One who understands much displays a greater simplicity of character than one who understands little.   ALEXANDER CHASE

He who calls in the aid of an equal understanding doubles his own. EDMUND BURKE

I hear and I forget; I see and I remember; I do and I understand. CHINESE PROVERB

Most people are bothered by those passages in Scripture which they cannot understand; but as for me I always noticed that the passages in Scripture which trouble me are those which I do understand. MARK TWAIN

A clever man tells a woman he understands her—but a stupid one tries to prove it.

People who understand each other never fight.

Instead of putting others in their place, try putting yourself in their place.

Little boy to his sister, after being scolded by parents: "I'll never understand grown-ups if I live to be eight!"

A simple rule in dealing with those who are hard to get along with is to remember that this person is striving to assert his superiority; and you must deal with him from that point of view.
ALFRED ADLER

Great Spirit, help me to never judge another until I have walked two miles in his moccasins.

When rejecting the ideas of another, make sure you reject only the idea and not the person.

Vision

If you love sleep, you will end in
poverty. Keep your eyes open, and
there will be plenty to eat!

PROVERBS 20:13

———

Where there is no vision,
the people perish.

PROVERBS 29:18, KJV

Vision

At one time, a fellow with his ear to the ground was a politician. Now he's just somebody looking for a lost contact lens.

VAUGHN MONROE

Vision is the art of seeing things invisible.   JONATHAN SWIFT

To small-minded men, the Lord gives small things.

Whoever it was who searched the heavens with a telescope and found no God would not have found the human mind if he had searched the brain with a microscope.   GEORGE SANTAYANA

Eyes that look are common. Eyes that see are rare.

J. OSWALD SANDERS

A rock pile ceases to be a rock pile the moment a single man contemplates it, bearing within him the image of a cathedral.

ANTOINE DE SAINT-EXUPÉRY

A great mind is one that can forget or look beyond itself.

WILLIAM HAZLITT

He will shoot higher who shoots at the sun than he who aims at a tree.

I see America, not in the setting of a black night of despair ahead of us; I see America in the crimson light of a rising sun fresh from the burning creative hand of God. I see great days ahead, great days possible to men and women of vision.

CARL SANDBURG

When it comes to spotting the faults of others, too many people seem to have twenty-twenty vision.

Vote

When there is moral rot within a nation, its government topples easily. But with wise and knowledgeable leaders, there is stability.

PROVERBS 28:2

———

When the godly are in authority, the people rejoice. But when the wicked are in power, they groan.

PROVERBS 29:2

Vote

Where annual elections end, there slavery begins.

JOHN QUINCY ADAMS

A straw vote only shows which way the hot air blows.

O. HENRY

We preach the virtues of democracy abroad. We must practice its duties here at home. Voting is the first duty of democracy.　　LYNDON B. JOHNSON

Voter: "I wouldn't vote for you, if you were St. Peter himself!" Candidate: "If I were St. Peter, you wouldn't be in my district!"

The number one problem in our country is apathy—but no one seems to care!

An American will cross the ocean to fight for democracy but won't cross the street to vote in a national election.

Whenever a fellow tells me he's bipartisan I know he's going to vote against me.　　HARRY S. TRUMAN

Among free men there can be no successful appeal from the ballot to the bullet. . . . The ballot is stronger than the bullet.

ABRAHAM LINCOLN

The future of this republic is in the hands of the American voter.　　DWIGHT D. EISENHOWER

The secret ballot in America is the most sacred heritage which we have and that I have stood by. Even my wife doesn't know how I voted.　　NELSON A. ROCKEFELLER

Winners/Losers

The whole city celebrates when the
godly succeed [win]; they shout for
joy when the godless die.

PROVERBS 11:10

———

I strain to reach the end of the race
and receive the prize for which God,
through Christ Jesus, is calling us up
to heaven.

THE APOSTLE PAUL, PHILIPPIANS 3:14

Winners/Losers

Winners find ways to make things work. Losers find excuses for why things don't work.

I always turn to the sports page first. The sports page records people's accomplishments; the front page, nothing but man's failures. EARL WARREN

Wars may be fought with weapons, but they are won by men. It is the spirit of the men who follow and of the man who leads that gains the victory. GEORGE PATTON JR.

Winning is not a sometime thing; it's an all-time thing. You don't win once in a while; you don't do things once in a while; you do them right all the time. Winning is a habit. Unfortunately, so is losing. VINCE LOMBARDI

Missing is part of winning. GEORGE FOREMAN

Winners are people who aren't afraid to take a chance now and then. Losers sit around and wait for the odds to improve.

If you cannot win the race, make the one ahead of you break the record.

Losers bemoan and bewail their blunders; winners bounce back in spite of their bloopers and boners. WILLIAM A. WARD

Winners expect to win in advance. Life is a self-fulfilling prophecy.

The man who wins may have been counted out several times, but he didn't hear the referee. H. E. JANSEN

Wisdom

Tune your ears to wisdom, and
concentrate on understanding. For
the Lord grants wisdom!

PROVERBS 2:2, 6

―――

Whoever walks with the wise will
become wise; whoever walks with
fools will suffer harm.

PROVERBS 13:20

―――

Sensible people keep their eyes glued
on wisdom, but a fool's eyes wander
to the ends of the earth.

PROVERBS 17:24

―――

Words of true wisdom are as
refreshing as a bubbling brook.

PROVERBS 18:4

Wisdom

Wise men learn more from fools than fools from wise men.

CATO

A good deal of trouble has been caused in the world by too
much intelligence and too little wisdom.

It's a wise man who lives with money in the bank; it's a fool
who dies that way.

FRENCH PROVERB

A fool tells what he will do; a boaster tells what he has done; a
wise man does it and says nothing.

A fool says, "I can't"; a wise man says, "I'll try."

The wise learn from tragedy; the foolish merely repeat it.

MICHAEL NOVAK

Before God, we are equally wise—equally foolish.

ALBERT EINSTEIN

From the errors of others a wise man corrects his own.

PUBLIUS SYRUS

Wisdom is knowing less but understanding more.

Wisdom—common sense to an uncommon degree.

The road to wisdom? Well, it's plain and simple to express:
Err and err and err again but less and less and less.

PIET HEIN

Epitaph to Charles II
Here lies our Sovereign Lord, the King,
Whose word no man relies on,
Who never said a foolish thing,
Nor ever did a wise one.   JOHN WILMOT

As a man grows older and wiser, he talks less and says more.

Caution is the eldest child of wisdom.   VICTOR HUGO

When a man lacks wisdom
His mind is always restless,
And his senses are wild horses
Dragging the driver hither and thither.
But when he is full of wisdom
His mind is collected
And his senses become tamed horses
Obedient to the driver's will.

Wise words are sometimes spoken in jest, but many more
foolish ones are spoken in earnest.

There are four kinds of people: Those who know not, and
know not that they know not. These are foolish. Those who
know not, and know they know not. These are the simple, and
should be instructed. Those who know, and know not that
they know. These are asleep; wake them. Those who know,
and know they know. These are the wise; listen to them.
                                              ARAB PHILOSOPHER

The doorstep to the temple of wisdom is a knowledge of our
own ignorance.   CHARLES SPURGEON

He who is wiser than his boss should be careful to conceal it.

Words

The godly think before speaking; the
wicked spout evil words. Harsh words
stir up anger. Gentle words bring life
and health.

PROVERBS 15:28, 1, 4

The words of the wise keep
them out of trouble.

PROVERBS 14:3

A truly wise person uses few words; a
person with understanding is
even-tempered.

PROVERBS 17:27

Words

Don't stop to pick up the kind words you drop.

Man does not live by words alone, despite the fact that sometimes he has to eat them.

Words should be weighed, not counted.

Words cannot change the truth. Being in the right does not depend on having a loud voice.   ORIENTAL PROVERB

Tart words make no friends: a spoonful of honey will catch more flies than a gallon of vinegar.

Another form of wastefulness is expenditure of words beyond the income of ideas.

All words are pegs to hang ideas on.   HENRY WARD BEECHER

A word is dead when it is said, some say. I say it just begins to live that day.   EMILY DICKINSON

Words once spoken can never be recalled.   WENTWORTH DILLON

Sharp words make more wounds than surgeons can heal.

Words are the most powerful drug used by mankind.
                                      RUDYARD KIPLING

Always keep your words soft and sweet—one day you may have to eat them.

Yesterday/Today/ Tomorrow

Teach us to make the most of our
time, so that we may grow in wisdom.

PSALM 90:12

———

Don't brag about tomorrow,
since you don't know what
the day will bring.

PROVERBS 27:1

Yesterday/Today/Tomorrow

As the years go by, they go quickly indeed;
Once over the hill, they pick up speed.

Years do not come to be counted; they come to count.

No matter how I used yesterday, I received twenty-four hours today.

Yesterday is gone; forget it! Tomorrow never comes; don't wait for it. Today is here; use it!

The man who wastes today lamenting yesterday will waste tomorrow lamenting today. PHILIP BASKIN

Today is the blessed time of rest you would have enjoyed if only you had done yesterday the things you were supposed to do the day before.

I have no yesterdays,
    Time took them all away.
Tomorrow may not be
    But I still have today.

Lament: I'm just catching up with yesterday. By tomorrow, I should be ready for today!

Today is nature's way of giving yesterday one more chance.

Happy the man, and happy he alone,
    He who can call today his own;
He who, secure within, can say,
    Tomorrow, do your worst,
For I have lived today.

Tomorrow is usually the busiest day of the year.

The lazier a man is, the more he plans to do tomorrow.

Did you hear about the fellow who faced his problems one tomorrow at a time?

One day is worth a thousand tomorrows.   BENJAMIN FRANKLIN

It is but a few short years from diapers to dignity and from dignity to decomposition.   DON HEROLD

Never put off until tomorrow what you can do today. If you wait until tomorrow, they will probably have passed a law prohibiting it.

Six-thirty is my time to rise,
    But I'm seldom bright of eye;
Part of me says, "Look alive!"
    And the other part asks, "Why?"

A small decision now can change all your tomorrows.
    ROBERT SCHULLER

Satan doesn't care how spiritual your intentions may be as long as they're focused on tomorrow.

Many find that things can be done in a day if they don't always make that day tomorrow.

Luxury is building tomorrows, living todays, and cherishing yesterdays.

Defer not until tomorrow to be wise, for tomorrow's sun for you may never rise.

I recommend you take care of the minutes: for hours will take care of themselves. Lord Chesterfield

Tomorrow is the most important thing in life. It comes into us at midnight very clean. It's perfect when it arrives and puts itself in our hands. It hopes we've learned something from yesterday. John Wayne

Tomorrow: the day when idlers work, and fools reform, and mortal men lay hold of heaven. Edward Young

Youth

A youngster's heart is filled
with foolishness, but discipline
will drive it away.

PROVERBS 22:15

———

Don't let the excitement of youth
cause you to forget your Creator.
Honor him in your youth before you
grow old and no longer enjoy living.

ECCLESIASTES 12:1

———

Young people who obey the law are
wise; those who seek out worthless
companions bring shame to their
parents. Robbing your parents
and then saying, "What's wrong
with that?" is as serious as
committing murder.

PROVERBS 28:7, 24

Youth

Youth is a wonderful thing. What a crime to waste it on children.
GEORGE BERNARD SHAW

We are only young once. That is all society can stand.
BOB BOWEN

Money isn't everything, but it sure keeps you in touch with the kids.

If you want to recapture your youth, just cut off his allowance.
AL BERNSTEIN

You are young at any age if you're planning for tomorrow.

All that steam you see is caused by young people trying to set on fire a world that is all wet.

Age is the best possible fire extinguisher for flaming youth.

You are young only once. If you act foolish after that, you'll have to find some other excuse.

Youth and beauty fade; character endures forever.

The worst danger that confronts the younger generation is the example set by the older generation.

Reputation is something to live up to in your youth and to live down in your old age.

A young man spends at least twelve years in school learning the English language; then he becomes a husband and never gets a chance to use it.

Two good openings for a young man are the legs in a pair of overalls.

How far a young man goes these days depends on how much gas is left in the car.

Why don't all challenges occur when we're seventeen and know everything?

Youth is a marvelous period of life. What a pity so many don't know what to do with it!

Next time you want to be young again, remember algebra.

Youth is not a time of life, it's a state of mind. You are as young as your faith, as old as your doubt; as young as your self-confidence, as old as your fear; as young as your hope, as old as your despair.

The key to success, according to today's youth, is the one that fits the ignition.

He who wants people to bet on him needs to have a good track record.

He aimed for happiness but settled for success.

The best device for clearing the driveway of snow is a youth who wants to use the car.

Nearly every man is a firm believer in heredity until his son makes a fool of himself.

To stay youthful, stay useful.

In youth, the days are short and the years are long; in old age, the years are short and the days long.

A pedestrian is a man with a car and a sixteen-year-old son.

One of the most difficult problems faced by a young man leaving home for the first time is giving up the fringe benefits.
MARGUERITE WHITLEY MAY